Create CALM™ From Chaos

⊗⊗⊗⊗⊗⊗⊗⊗⊗

7 Steps to Maximize Power, Performance and Profits

Laurie K. Grant

Published by
Laurie K. Grant
Toronto, Ontario, Canada

Copyright © 2017 by Laurie K. Grant
Toronto, Ontario, CANADA

1st EDITION

ISBN: 978-1-77277-142-8

LaurieKGrant.com | CreateCalmFromChaos.com

For information about special discounts for bulk purchases, please contact LaurieKGrant.com

TABLE OF CONTENTS

TABLE OF FIGURES

FOREWORD

I'm Raymond Aaron, the top ten New York Times Bestselling Author of the books Branding Small Business For Dummies, Double Your Income Doing What You Love, Chicken Soup for the Parent's Soul and Chicken Soup for the Canadian Soul. I have been a real estate investor, a business mentor and coach for over 30 years. I have shared the stage with former President Bill Clinton, Sir Ricard Branson, Donald Trump, Steve Wozniak, and many other world-class leaders and speakers. I have dedicated my life to teaching people like you how to dramatically change your life for the better by helping you to tap into your potential.

There are countless books on business in the marketplace today, but Laurie K. Grant's **Create CALM From Chaos**™ is the one book you don't want to be without. Why? This book is worth thousands of hours of your time and is full of comprehensive strategies to use to make more money for your business. It's concise, well-written, and insightful. I highly recommend **Create CALM From Chaos**™, an approach this book describes in detail.

When you read **Create CALM From Chaos**™ and follow the ideas presented to you, you save thousands of hours of wasted time. You learn how to keep your business running in a structured, organized way which allows you to focus on what you do best and to provide **WOW** experiences for your clients, your employees, and even your vendors. Every page of this book is overflowing with extensive approaches, which are simple to understand and easy to implement.

Create CALM From Chaos™ covers everything you need to know to simplify and systemize your business, including why you need to get organized, how to cope effectively with the fear of change, what to do to manage your time (you will be surprised how you do this), and your work environment. Laurie reveals how to run projects, how to manage your data (business information), and most importantly, how to manage people: your clients, your employees, and your vendors. She shares important areas of your business finances, ways to increase your knowledge, and how to create an organized, structured (systemized) framework for you to operate your business.

In 2013, I had the pleasure of being introduced to Laurie K. Grant because she attended one of my events. I have since learned she is an incredibly intelligent, clever, and powerful woman who is very determined and extremely successful at anything she focuses her mind on. Laurie is a true entrepreneurial spirit with more than 20 years' international experience delivering business transformation solutions for Fortune Top 50 corporations, multi-nationals, mid-sized businesses, and startups, Laurie is esteemed by her clients and colleagues for an unprecedented ability to assess any challenge at hand generating the most innovative and sustainable solution.

I'm **WOWED** by Laurie K. Grant and her unique ability to **Create CALM From Chaos**™, and I know you will be too.

Raymond Aaron
New York Times Bestselling Author

Author of:
Branding Small Business For Dummies
Double Your Income Doing What You Love
Chicken Soup for the Parent's Soul
Chicken Soup for the Canadian Soul

DEDICATION

I write this dedication to the three people who I know without a shadow of a doubt believe in me. I am deeply honoured to have them be a part of my life and my memories.

First and foremost, **Dr. Harold Laurier Grant**, the man who chose me at age three when my mother no longer wanted me, the man who I called Daddy and who I am named after. He was a lifelong learner with a keen interest in nature, science, and truth. He was my knight in shining armour who always encouraged me to be the very best me. I loved to mentally spar with him on Physics vs. Quantum Physics vs. Metaphysics.

Secondly, **Harley Jaymes Grant**, my son who has taught me many things about life. He was to be my birthday present, but came earlier just to surprise me. Harley has a keen interest in art and psychology intersecting in the human experience. It's been a delight to share my life with one who is my intellectual equal and who isn't afraid to challenge the status quo.

The third and final person is my dear friend, **Carla Wynn Hall**. She was the catalyst to show me I needed to share my brilliance with the world and by not doing so, I wasn't in service. Carla has a keen interest in the art of storytelling, not only to keep culture alive for years to come, but to use the craft of putting pen to paper as a means to heal the wounds held within.

THE LAW OF ONENESS

Without you —my journey is less
Without you – I have less yes
Without you – I'm not the best me
Without you – I may never be free

THANK YOU

May My Brilliance Shine to Light Your Way

CHAPTER 1

WHY SYSTEMIZE YOUR BUSINESS?

☙❧☙❧☙❧☙❧☙❧

Join Me on the SYSTEMIZATION Journey

Glad to see you stopped in. Are you ready for some tough love? In these next pages, you will either recognize yourself or someone you know. You may not like some of the things I'm going to tell you in my book, but I'm not going to walk softly. In fact, I'm going to be blunt and direct. Why? Because the reason you bought my book is you already know in your heart of hearts you need to get organized, structured, and focused or in other words **SYSTEMIZED**. Especially because you want to grow your business to the next level and beyond.

SYSTEM = Save Yourself, Stress, Time, Energy & Money

You've watched others grow their business to success, but you're not getting ahead. In fact, you've lost business and yet you still don't take any steps to change. Why did you start your business? You started your business because you:

- Have a great idea you want to share with the world.
- Want to have more control over how you work.
- Want more work life balance.
- Want to make more money, etc.

Whatever the reason is, you didn't start a business to be a failure. You started a business to be a **SUCCESS**, but you find success alluding you.

It's time for a little tough love. Get **SYSTEMIZED** like yesterday! You like winning, don't you? Well, you're the only one who to make this happen. The only one to make the changes you need for your business. Don't put it off anymore. Do it **NOW**!! With my guidance in this book, you will get organized, structured, and focused. You will be **SYSTEMIZED** and able to move your business forward. Why get **SYSTEMIZED**? Systems are regularly repeated patterns. By using them you will **WOW** your clients, your employees, your vendors, and yourself.

Today, more and more entrepreneurs are breaking ground with bright new ideas. They're innovative and intuitive with brilliant concepts, but they lack one major asset: systems. This book will teach you in easy steps, how to create systems for your business to allow you to be more organized, more structured, and more focused on what you do best. You will learn how to create flexible, repeatable and easy to put into play sustainable systems. Then you're able to focus on what's important to you – **Your Business**.

This book is written for you, to help guide you, to help you be more successful in your business. You don't have to read this book from front to back – why you ask? You may only need help in one area, then jump to the particular area you're interested in to see what tips and guidance are there. Read it back to front, from the middle outwards; it doesn't really matter which way you read it, as long as you read it. Are you ready? Get set, let's begin. Together we will move through the process of taking your brilliant creation into the world.

Why listen to me? I'm the Premier International Business Strategy and Efficiency Expert, Award Winning and International Bestselling Author, Global Speaker and Thought Leader. I'm the Founder and CEO of FutureWave Group Inc., a consulting company that designs and implements business transformation solutions for organizations including Fortune Top 50 corporations, multi-nationals, mid-sized businesses, start-ups, and entrepreneurs. I lead the day-to-day responsibilities, including client consultations, managing projects, and everything in between. Over the last 20 years, I've worked with organizations such as EDS, IBM, Blue Cross, Anheuser Busch, Enbridge Gas, various Canadian Federal and Provincial Ministries, RBC, CIBC, York University, Dow Jones, ADP, Funddata, Debi/Davidge, and General Motors to name a few. I have two degrees. One degree is in Information Technology with a minor in Professional and Technical Writing. The second degree is in Electronics Engineering Technology – Control Systems.

This makes me well qualified to help you bring **CALM** to your business. Are you ready for this adventure? Yes. Alright then, let's get started.

Business Chaos Analysis™

Please select the boxes below when the questions are applicable to you. It's my passion to help you find the **CALM** in your Chaos by creating easy, sustainable systems so your business works for you. Let's have a conversation to see how we can bring **CALM** to your business. Go to BreakTheChaos.com to start the journey and in a few minutes, you'll be directed to my calendar to select a date and time for you.

Framework
- ☐ Do you know where to start or what to focus on to create your business?
- ☐ Do you make constant changes in your business, but they're not bringing you the desired results?
- ☐ Are you repeating the same activities over and over because you don't have a business plan?
- ☐ Do you reinvent the wheel each time you execute an activity?
- ☐ Do you have the structure or the system to support you, so you will focus on your great ideas?

Change
- ☐ Do you find you're scattered as you jump from one great idea to the next?
- ☐ Do you want control of your business direction, but don't know how to achieve it?
- ☐ Are you reactive, not proactive, always chasing the fires to put out?
- ☐ Do you see everything as an emergency?
- ☐ Are you doing everything yourself as you don't know how to delegate?

Time
- ☐ Are you overwhelmed despite achieving some business growth and success?
- ☐ Do you find you don't have enough hours in the day?
- ☐ Do you find you don't have work-life balance as you're spending all your time on your business?
- ☐ Do you find you don't undertake additional business to enhance your business or excite you?
- ☐ Are you doing activities that don't belong to your business?

Environment
- ☐ Are you aware of the ongoing changes in your competition?
- ☐ Are you aware of the competitive products and/or services in the marketplace?
- ☐ Have you stopped marketing or advertising because of a lack of funds?
- ☐ Are your products and/or services outdated?
- ☐ Do you have a chaotic work environment?

Clients
- ☐ Is your business plagued with losing your existing clients?
- ☐ Are you attracting the wrong clients for you?
- ☐ Are you creating work for your clients that isn't complete or has errors?
- ☐ Do you know and clearly communicate what your business is selling?
- ☐ Do you ask for and listen to client feedback?

Money
- ☐ Have you mixed your business money in with your personal money?
- ☐ Does your business have a budget?
- ☐ Do you have a business budget, but you don't stick to it?
- ☐ Did your business expenses increase, but you haven't raised your prices?
- ☐ Have you got the cash flow to sustain your business cycle?

Technology
- ☐ Do you understand technology and how it improves your business?
- ☐ Do you know how to use Social Media for marketing your business?
- ☐ Do you understand Social Media platforms like Facebook, Twitter, LinkedIn or Instagram?
- ☐ Do you have a website, but terms like SEO or mobile friendly confuse you?
- ☐ Do you know how to reach a virtual audience and have virtual conversations like Skype or Google Hangout?

What Does Business Failure Look Like?

It's important you understand what business failure is to avoid going down this road. Business failure is getting stuck in a rut, going around and around in circles, not able to move forward, not generating enough revenue to take care of your expenses, and not having any profit. There are many reasons for business failure: lack of funding or money, changes in the economic marketplace, ineffective business management, poor employee behaviour, and high employee turnover, to name just a few. Ineffective business management is often seen in poor planning or a lack of know-how to recognize what's required to operate a prosperous business.

Your business fails when you don't understand and know your marketplace and who your target clients are. It's important to know who your competition is and what your clients are buying. You need to arm yourself with as much information about your competition and your clients regularly to position yourself in the most advantageous light. You need to be flexible to changes in either your competition or your clients.

Just because you have a bright shiny idea doesn't mean you will have a highly profitable business. You want to choose products and/or services to achieve growth. Your cash register must ring. It takes more than a great idea and your passion to make your business a success.

Much like an airplane, start-up businesses are born from a bright idea. Women, particularly, have what many perceive as flighty ideas. Ideas which have great energy and momentum. These ideas are needed just like the jet fuel a 747 jet needs to take flight; self-sufficient entrepreneurs have a million ideas. Not only do they have great ideas, they spend countless dollars to learn about different ways to create businesses. They attend endless classes in programs presented by industry gurus. There comes a point in time, however, when a condition called "Failure to Launch" inflicts the plan, dismantles the dreams, and causes a good business idea to become a retired business idea; one that is never born.

Many times, a business is launched and it enjoys a nice take-off, starts making money, but then a shift occurs. Like the economy crashes as in the 2008 US Real Estate Crash, or technology changes as it does often. Either one of these variables, when injected into a business model, causes **Chaos** of the mind and break down in the business. This is what happens when a business has failed to create flexible strategies to keep up with potential shifts in the marketplace. When creating the concept of systemized **CALM** from an event of **Chaos**, it's important to account for those "unknown" variables" by developing a futuristic "What If" situation to mitigate "Failure to Land." Landing in this context means longevity and stability.

Let's look at some common things I've seen time and time again in my clients' businesses to see what might cause your business to fail.

Do you know and clearly communicate what your business is selling? What is the value you provide to your clients? Is there enough cash flow to sustain your business cycle? You must keep the cash register ringing. Do you know of ways to increase the business income, reduce the expenses or get funding from grants, loans, partners or investors?

Are you aware of changes in the competition, or products in the marketplace, or new technologies to help you? How dependent are you on your clients? Don't put all your eggs in one basket. How well do you interact with your clients? Do you ask for and listen to client feedback? Do you say **NO**? Do you focus on delivering results that are over-the-top of what your clients expected? Do you give them the **WOW** factor? I will explain the **WOW** factor throughout the book.

Have you stopped marketing or advertising because of a lack of funds? This makes it more challenging to find more clients. What are some alternative strategies to use? Ask your clients how they found you each time you take on a new client. This gives you a targeted list to focus your marketing efforts on.

What are your social media strategies? Some places to direct your social media marketing efforts to are Facebook, LinkedIn, Twitter, Pinterest, Instagram, Periscope, etc. Getting feedback from your clients goes a long way in teaching you how to provide not just great service, but a service which gives them a **WOW** experience.

Is your inventory stale? Has your inventory been on the shelf too long? Is your inventory out of date with what your clients want? If you answered yes to any of these questions, then lower your prices and sell your inventory at a discount to make room for products your clients do want. Do you survey your clients to find out what are the latest trends they're interested in? The responses provide you with market research.

How often are your employees leaving and you're having to replace them with new hires? Are you not paying them enough? Are they not passionately involved with the work they're doing? Is the work they're doing is too easy and they're bored? Employees like **WOW** experiences too.

Did your business expenses increase, but you haven't raised your prices? Guess what this does, it eats into your profitability which doesn't give you the funding to make your business grow and prosper. What are you doing to fix this? Look at increasing your prices, finding cheaper vendors, or different products to offer your clients.

What is your health like? Do you get emotional because you're overwhelmed? Do you overreact to every little thing that happens in your business? It's important to get enough sleep, food, exercise, and spiritual space or you become too tired or have headaches or get fatigued mentally. Have you set personal and professional boundaries in your business? Are you unable to grow your business to the next level as you're worn out with doing everything?

You have to maintain a variety of activities to successfully run a business. When you don't plan, organize, control, direct or communicate, you run the risk of failure. You need to know exactly where your business is at any given moment. As you start to grow, you must plan to change. Failure to anticipate change is inviting your business to fail. If you keep on doing the same thing, you will keep on getting the same results. A strategic map will tell you where your business was yesterday, where your business is today, and where your business is going tomorrow. Are you up for the challenge?

You will fail at some things you do in your business, but when you know your business like a captain does his ship, then you will adjust and change as the business climate changes. Failure leads to growth and ultimately success.

Understanding the State of Business Chaos

What is Chaos?

The Oxford Dictionaries describe the meaning for **Chaos** as "complete disorder and confusion." The word originated in the 15th century (denoting a gaping void or chasm, later formless primordial matter): via French and Latin from the Greek *khaos,* vast chasm, void.

> *"It's a lack of clarity that creates chaos and frustration.*
> *Those emotions are poison to any living goal."*
> Steve Maraboli, Life, the Truth, and Being Free

Chaos is defined in many ways, but in business it's defined as a slow, painful death. You know, the death that happens when **Chaos** overtakes normalcy and keeps a business in a constant, spiralling state of stuck.

Allowing **Chaos** to take up residence in your business brings failure when you don't have a way to manage the **Chaos** and to create a structured, focused, systemized order. In today's business world, as a busy entrepreneur, you find yourself in a total state of overwhelm, creating confusion, mayhem, and disorder in your business. This state of **Chaos** contributes to you feeling you're not in control, you're being swallowed up in a vortex and you're isolated from your great idea.

> *"Chaos is a name for any order that produces confusion in our minds."*
> George Santayana, Dominations and Powers

This book provides you with ideas to assist you in creating sustainable solutions for your business. Many new or growing entrepreneurs feel totally lost in a sea of confusion and critically disjointed **Chaos**. **Chaos** puts you into a state of disharmony and disconnection from your business venture. To be successful, you cannot jump on the bandwagon of every impulse that comes to mind.

Create CALM From Chaos^{TM} is written to assist you with creating the bridge to connect a bright idea to a moneymaking business. This model is centred on organized management, implementing systems, and the importance of compartmentalizing ideas into profit generating activities critical in today's market. We're in a knowledge revolution today and there is no getting around this fact. Rapid amounts of change occur constantly in today's world, providing new technologies, along with new ways of thinking and being. To stay on top of this change, you and your team must learn to bend and adjust quickly, allowing you to manoeuvre your business through the sea of volatility.

You need to learn the signs of **Chaos** in your business so you adapt and change as required. Losing clients, employees, or vendors; health problems; not enough time in the day; no time for yourself or your loved ones; overspending; not enough money; etc. These are signs you're in a **State of Chaos.**

Having **Chaos** in your mind puts limits on your ability to focus and to clearly process information. Neuroscientists at Princeton University have discovered **Chaos** competes for your brain's attention, resulting in less focus and more stress.

This **Chaos** isn't just physical, it's also digital and mental. Your to-do list, your email, Twitter, Facebook, and texting all create **Chaos**. Constant interruptions overwhelm your brain and it doesn't work, it doesn't filter, it doesn't process, and you become overwhelmed.

When you stay in this state of **Chaos** for any length of time, it starts to adversely affect your life, your health, your relationships, your career or your business. Therefore, it's extremely important for you to learn ways to master your chaos, to **Create CALM From Chaos**™.

What Does Business Success Look Like?

It's important to understand what business success is so you recognize when you're on the right path. Success is defined differently for everyone. In business, there are a few signposts to tell you when you're on the successful road. Your business makes money, it's profitable and growing, or it's the feelings of satisfaction and pride from the problems you solved, or the clients you served.

Success is peace of mind because you've done your absolute best. Success is knowing the core values of your business are in alignment with the core values you live by. Success is knowing you're passionate about what you do and it's highly enjoyable so it becomes play for you. Success is because you don't quit, you pick yourself up, you change yourself and your business, and you do it with enthusiasm. Fully immersing yourself in your business brings you great joy and personal satisfaction.

How do you measure the success of your business? Are you mindful of your goals and targets, ensuring they are aligned with the values and purpose of your business? Have you got plans written down for your business? Do you have a blueprint of your business vision; what your business goals and drivers are? Without a roadmap, you cannot drive from Point A to Point B. The same is true in your business.

When you first start your business, your business plan is small. Revisit your business plan at least once a year. Make it a living, growing document that tracks how you change your business. To be successful, you need to understand all aspects of your business. Make sure you delegate the tasks others are able to do, leaving you with the tasks only you're able to do to make your cash register ring.

Some Examples of Business Success
Profit - Most people believe business profit is one of the best ways to measure your business success. Here are some other good ways to measure business success:

- When you're making money after your expenses are paid.
- When you have money to reinvest in your business.
- When your money and your business are continually growing.

Clients - The number of new clients you bring in shows how you successfully communicate with your target market. Happy clients will be repeat clients and they will provide great referrals for you. Make sure you provide your clients with a **WOW** experience right from the first time they interact with you and your business. Always remember, the client is the most important. Without your clients, you have no business. Make sure you have great client service.

Employees - Give your employees a work environment that fosters their professional growth, applauds their achievements, and makes them feel valued for their efforts. A happy, satisfied employee is more likely to bend over backwards for you, your business, your clients, and your vendors. Remember, your employees need **WOW** experiences too.

Vendors - Paying your vendors ahead of time or on time is one of the best ways to have happy vendors. Be open about what you need and what your business goals are. Develop the relationship. Work towards a mutual benefit. Build on candidness, honesty, and integrity. Choose vendors you believe share your visions and your values. The quality of your products and/or service depends on the quality of your vendors.

You - The most important person to keep happy, engaged, and valued is yourself. You set an example for your business, your clients, your employees, and your vendors. That's why it's important for you to do reality checks regularly to make sure your business is on the right track and, if not, make the required changes.

Understanding the State of Business Calm

On the opposite end of **Chaos** is **CALM**. **CALM** in your business is peaceful, quiet, and without worry. The state of being organized and prepared for business transactions, from organizing finances to creating a marketing plan that flows with the changing times. While having a structured, focused, systemized business may be painful for the entrepreneur who is flying with ideas, it helps increase your business profits in the long run. When **CALM** is achieved, or at least moved to the top of the line, a business will flow smoother.

What is Calm?

The Oxford Dictionaries describe the meaning for **CALM** as "tranquil and quiet." The word originated from Late Middle English: via one of the Romance languages from the Greek *kauma* 'heat (of the day)'.

CALM is defined in many ways, but in business it's defined as a smoothly functioning growing organization. You know, the state that happens when **CALM** is present every day in your business. You have a plan, you're focused, and you're consistent in the delivery of your products and/or services, yet flexible enough to manage change. This means your clients feel understood. Your clients know you're taking care of them. They not only keep coming back, but they also refer you to other clients.

As the captain of your ship, you know your priorities for the direction you're taking your business in. Your processes are stable, your clients are happy, your employees are engaged, your vendors deliver great products on time and, best of all, the cash register is ringing. Trust, integrity, focus, discipline, and perseverance are part of your value system. You're organized, you keep detailed records to know exactly where your business is at all times, you're learning from your competition, you've analysed the pros and cons of the calculated risks to grow your business, and you're open to new ideas and ways for your business to run.

"When adversity strikes, that's when you have to be the most calm. Take a step back, stay strong, stay grounded and press on."
LL Cool J

When you invest in your business, your clients, your employees, and your vendors, you're also investing in yourself. You're accessible, you have a great reputation, you're an expert in your field, and you market the benefits of having your products and/or services. You know your target market and what's important to them. You stay in touch, you over deliver and ahead of time, you say thank you, you answer emails and phone calls, and you do it all with a smile.

This is a great place to be. You have mastered **Chaos**. You've created Business **CALM** from your Business **Chaos**. If this is **You**, congratulations!!! However, with this book, you will learn something new, a fresh perspective you didn't have before. If this is **Not You**, don't worry, you're going to move forward. The 1st step was in buying this book, in believing I'm able to help you, which I can. I've helped many organizations over the years and I want to help **YOU** to have financial abundance, personal freedom, and significant success while providing **WOW** experiences for your clients, your employees, and your vendors.

Let's take a look at some of the changes to lead you on a path to financial abundance, personal freedom and significant success. In the next chapter, we will look at **Change** and how it affects you, your business, your clients, your employees, and your vendors. I provide tips and tools I've used successfully with my clients, my employees and my vendors to **Create CALM From Chaos**™.

CHAPTER 2

UNDERSTANDING CHANGE

ೞ౭౩౬ೞ౭౩౬

What is Change?

Change is moving from your present business state (how your business is today) through a transient business state to a new business state (how you envision or want your business to be). Change is a common factor in life. You cannot escape change. Change happens all around us and is either directed internally or externally. Change is either major or minor. Change is either anticipated or unexpected. Whatever the change is, it's always a progression from a current business state through a transient business state to a new business state.

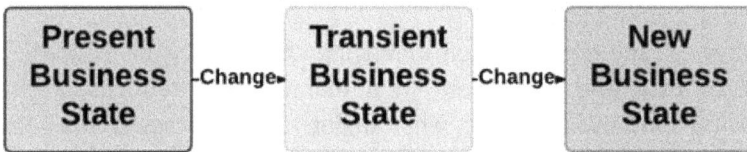

Present Business State	-Change-	Transient Business State	-Change-	New Business State

Figure 1- States of Change

Change takes you out of your comfort zone. Change has an adjustment period, which varies from business to business. Change is uncomfortable, for changing from one state to the next takes away your control over your expected outcomes. This is where being flexible is important. You need to employ change when the current state of your business is no longer working for you, when it's no longer growing and hopefully, you put this into motion before change takes you on a downward spiral. Change is difficult when not managed.

Who Does Change Affect

Changes are required in your business when you decide you want to improve your business performance, or seize new opportunities, or address strategic issues. These changes affect:

- Your business processes – the way work is done.
- Your clients – who receive the work.
- Your employees – who do the work.
- Your vendors – who assist in the work.

Change affects the people around your business. They have to ultimately change as your business changes. However, your employees are the most affected by any change. When your employees aren't given the necessary support to manage the change, the change fails. Your employees cannot become champions of a change in your business unless they see you, their fearless leader, as the change champion.

There's always discomfort in uncertainty or transitioning from one state to the next. Today's world has rising uncertainty from global impacts on finance and economics. When you focus on this state, it leads you to have a short-term or reactive focus. It's imperative you don't allow yourself and your business to get stuck here. Continue to work your business plan to build value. Stay away from bad news.

I always tell my clients, when managing change in your business, you want to plan and implement in a manner that reduces employee opposition and business cost, while taking full advantage of the value of your change effort. Your business may have to undergo constant changes to stay competitive in today's world.

This example shows you how to manage change and be proactive with your clients.

At one time, I worked in a business that provided customized data mappings for a number of clients. The data mappings were made using EDI (Electronic Data Interchange) standards. I implemented a process that, whenever a standard changed, we'd search our client database to find out who had the standard or who had a customized mapping which used the standard. These changes usually were a change to the technical layout or a change to the way a field was used by one of their EDI partners.

By contacting our clients immediately, we saved them significant time and money as they knew ahead of time how they and their business partners are affected. They now implement the necessary changes more effectively and efficiently. This added real value to our clients and provided us with great client loyalty and retention.

Why Change is Difficult?

It's Unknown – We're conditioned to fear what is unfamiliar or unknown.

It's Challenging – Change takes you into new areas, testing your abilities.

It's Emotional – Change shakes us out of our familiar routines.

Most people like the familiar; driving the same route to work every day, doing the same tasks at work, these provide a psychological safety net. When you introduce change, it creates insecurity. You must understand these factors about change and address them in your change management plan.

Even you, as the fearless leader of your business, are subject to resistance after you've made the decision to introduce change in your business. You remember the little voice in your head, the one that nags and doubts – you have to be vigilant to acknowledge and quiet the little voice.

When you introduce change it impacts the culture of your business with your clients, your employees, and your vendors. You must understand you're dealing with different personalities. Understanding how they're motivated is key to keeping them involved in the change and moving forward.

Change costs you time, money, and energy to travel from your current state through a transitory state to arrive at the future state you desire. Yet you must change your business time and time again, because if you don't and you continually do what you have always done, then you continually get what you've always got, and your business stagnates or even worse, fails.

Humans become emotionally attached to their lives, some more than others. Any change, even one that means new and great things for your business, means the removal of something familiar and valued. It's really helpful for you to understand the behaviour models for how humans manage the stages of change and/or grief and to adapt contingencies for managing these stages in your Change Management plan.

As the fearless leader of your business, you need to help the people who are affected by the change in your business to feel secure by addressing their concerns. How do you do this, you ask? Great question – involve those people affected by the change in the change process, consult with them, listen to their ideas – make them part of your business change journey.

I tell my clients you cannot impose change on your people, you will be seen as a dictator. This doesn't build loyalty. Bring your people into the change journey by having them be active participants. Change is not transactional, it's transformational. You need to understand human psychology and address your people's real concerns. These concerns are usually about how the change is going to affect them. Make people see how positive this change is and how negative not changing will be. Develop your soft skills to sell this effectively. You require the ability to empathize and walk in their shoes.

You cannot just communicate to the people connected to your business that there is a change coming, you must also put into place the tools which will help to implement the change. This is especially important when your change involves changing your business culture. Hiring a coach to help with the change is beneficial. You most certainly want to involve your people in the change.

Face Everything and Rise

Most people talk about **FEAR** as danger, something to be avoided, or something to be afraid of. **FEAR** affects the decisions you make. **FEAR** is governed by your reptilian brain, which is the area of your brain that wants to keep you safe. When your brain has gone into **FEAR** mode, you won't explore new options or take risks. **FEAR** shuts you down before you even get started. I prefer to see **FEAR** as **Face Everything and Rise.**

The **Fear of Change** is called Metathesiophobia. The origin of the word Metathesiophobia comes from Greek 'meta' meaning **change** and phobos meaning **fear.**

"Failure is the key to success; each mistake teaches us something."
Morihei Ueshiba

Change is difficult because it causes us to behave in a different way than the normal. Change is chaotic when you move things around and suddenly feel like you don't know where the pieces go. Change is tough when you're required to work your way out of a produced problem. Change is trying because it taps into emotions. Change is frustrating when you haven't done the internal work and you have rigid requirements of yourself or others. Change takes you out of your comfort zone, which is very uncomfortable as humans are creatures of habit and slow to take action

The **Fear of Failure** is called Atychiphobia. It's a type of specific phobia that is abnormal, unwarranted, and persistent. As with many phobias, atychiphobia often leads to a constricted lifestyle, and is particularly devastating for its effects on a person's willingness to attempt certain activities.

> *"Only those who dare to fail greatly can ever achieve greatly."*
> Robert F. Kennedy

The fear of failing brings your business to a halt. You end up doing nothing and therefore your business isn't moving forward. When fear has found its way into your life, it stops you from moving in a forward progression and means you miss some truly great opportunities. Quite often it's not the fear of failing that overtakes you, but what you perceive as the negative outcomes such as not having the business income or being embarrassed. You believe you look like a fool and usually this is only in your head.

> *"Fear is only as deep as the mind allows."*
> Japanese Proverb

The **Fear of Success** is called Achievemephobia. While it may seem strange to you, it's actually a very real social phobia, which prevents you from achieving your business goals.

> *"Success is not final; failure is not fatal:*
> *it is the courage to continue that counts."*
> Winston Churchill

Do you have a fear of success? Do you have a lot of recurring negative things occurring in your life? Such as you've finally gotten out of debt and then boom, something happens to your financial picture. Or you're great at getting clients, but you cannot keep them and you're having trouble building client loyalty. You're working really hard, but you have no traction, your business is just full of busy work. Or you have what I call the rabbit syndrome – remember the white rabbit from Alice's Adventures in Wonderland? – I'm late, I'm late for a very important date. You're guilty of self-sabotage and don't even know it.

Types of Change

Many types of changes affect you, your business, your clients, your employees, and your vendors. It's important to understand the various types of change so you recognize them and manage them appropriately. You need to manage effectively as the complexity of the pace that ever-increasing change from immediate communication, global internet connection, email, cell phones, and other tools has on your life and your business is phenomenal.

"Our greatest glory is not in never falling,
but in rising every time we fall."
Confucius

Have you adjusted to new conditions without changing the way you execute your life or your business? Have you assumed the rules haven't changed, you just have to work smarter? Sometimes the rules shift and there is no announcement; it just happens and you look up to notice some people and their businesses are achieving new levels of success. They created a paradigm shift.

Business changes are driven by having your business acquired and merged into another company, by changes in leadership, or by changes in the marketplace, and when you don't adapt to these changes, your business fails.

Culture/People changes are aimed at changing the behaviour patterns of your employees in the areas of communication, motivation, interaction, and leadership. You use a variety of methods such as reward, recognition, empowerment, or training to assist in changing employee behaviours.

Leadership changes are important as they offer your business an opportunity to effect major changes. Strategic changes in people, policy, procedures, or structure are more easily introduced to your business at the time of a change in leadership.

Strategic changes cover many functional areas of your business. They usually focus on what you're doing to achieve your business goals, such as how you do business, the markets you do business in, what kinds of partnerships you have, your products and/or services, etc.

Technology changes affect the hardware or software systems you have in your business or the way you do business with your partners, your clients, your employees, and your vendors.

Process changes affect the way the work is brought into your business, performed in your business, and delivered to your clients. This type of change is for productivity improvement.

> *"Progress is impossible without change,*
> *and those who cannot change their minds cannot change anything."*
> George Bernard Shaw

Change is started by many different drivers. You experience change because of growth, downsizing, or relocating. Change is planned, unplanned, transactional, transformational, evolutionary, revolutionary, disruptive or innovative. Change happens to your business structure, technology, operational procedures, or your business culture. There are too many different types for me to list them all here, but the important point is to understand there are many different ways change in your business is triggered.

> *"Success is most often achieved by those who*
> *don't know that failure is inevitable."*
> Coco Chanel

Today your business needs to have more than just a purpose for being.

You need to be focused to lead your business and its resources to the best opportunities available, being aware that those opportunities change from day to day, week to week, month to month, and year to year. You must start with the end in mind. What are the results you're seeking? Is it increased sales, profits, happier clients, better services, etc.? You need to steer your business through the storms of the ever-changing marketplace; being focused, connecting and aligning all the parts of the puzzle to get you to the success you desire.

It helps to look at change as evolution. Your business is always evolving to meet the changes in the marketplace landscape. When you don't change, your business is like the plant in your garden that didn't get enough sun, water or nutrients and has withered and died. You don't want this for your business

Change Models

Change models are tools to streamline the change process and make it easier for you to apply the principles. I have picked a few I use with my clients to give you some ideas on how to manage change in your business.

The first one I will show you is the **CAISS**[TM] change management model – **C**ognition, **A**mbition, **I**nformation, **S**kill, **S**upport.

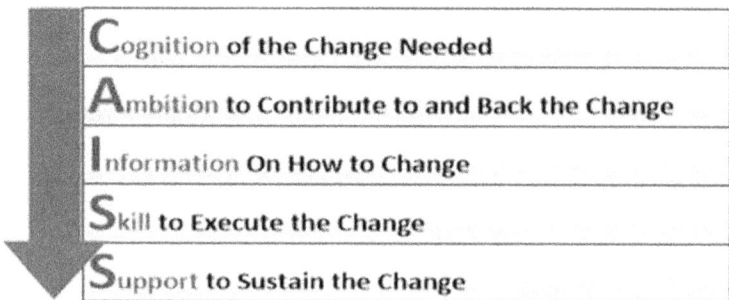

Cognition **of the Change Needed**
Ambition **to Contribute to and Back the Change**
Information **On How to Change**
Skill **to Execute the Change**
Support **to Sustain the Change**

Figure 2 - CAISS[TM] Change Management Model

1. **Cognition of the Change Needed.** This stage is when you're cognizant of the need to change. You need to know why the change is required. Early communication to understand the change is key

here.

2. **Ambition to Contribute to and Back the Change.** This stage requires building the ambition to be involved in the change.

3. **Information on How to Change.** This stage requires information transference about the change using coaching, education, mentoring, training, and forums. Two important aspects here: how to execute the change and how to perform after the change.

4. **Skill to Execute the Change.** This stage is the skill to execute the change. Performance is supported through practice, coaching, and feedback.

5. **Support to Sustain the Change.** This last stage supports the change by feedback, reward, recognition, performance measurement, and using corrective action when required.

The second model I will show you is the **RAS**™ change management model – **Release, Adjust, Set.**

Figure 3 - RAS™ Change Management Model

1. **RELEASE** – is a stage of release, of preparation, and organization to change, knowing the change is necessary. Deadlines are important to push you into a trajectory propelling the change forward. Here you look at the change pros and cons. When the pros outweigh the cons, make the change.

2. **ADJUST** – is an adjustment stage as the change is executed. This is the scariest part of the change. Give support such as training, coaching, and flexibility with errors. Providing change role models and being open to other people creating solutions is helpful. Communicate a clear picture of the change and the benefits so everyone involved knows where they are heading.

3. **SET** – is a hardening stage after the change has occurred.

Acceptance has occurred and new routines are established. However, this doesn't mean there won't be other changes to manage at a different time.

Change Management

When initiating change in your business, you need to apply **Change Management** methods because any changes affect how you conduct your business, which in turn has an impact on your clients, your employees, and your vendors.

All the people involved in a change will manage the change in a variety of ways. Some people welcome change; others dislike it. Change makes some people happy; others are unhappy. Some people adapt quickly to a change; others are slow or resistant to any change.

"If you change the way you look at things,
the things you look at change."
Wayne Dyer

Change Management is a structured method for ensuring changes are methodical, easily applied, and the lasting benefits of change are realised. **Change Management** is a discipline to guide how you prepare and support successful change which drives business success and outcomes.

CHANGE MANAGEMENT STEPS

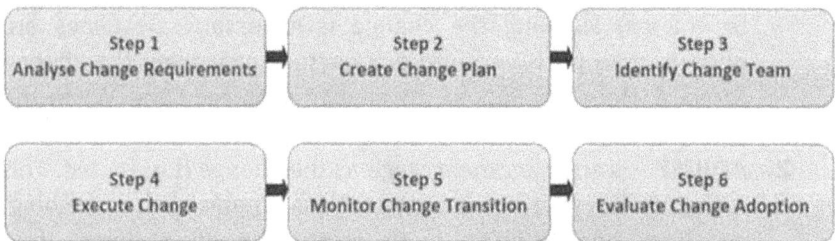

Step 1 Analyse Change Requirements	→	Step 2 Create Change Plan	→	Step 3 Identify Change Team
Step 4 Execute Change	→	Step 5 Monitor Change Transition	→	Step 6 Evaluate Change Adoption

Figure 4 - Change Management Steps

Communication from the top down is key in managing change. This means you, the fearless leader of your business, must be visibly seen as encouraging and communicating the positive benefits and results for your business.

Change Management is a planned and deliberate method for enabling the adoption of change by all those who are involved in the change. The important motives behind most transformations or changes in your business are going to be to increase revenues and/or profits, to decrease costs, or to become more effective and efficient. You have to change because your business is:

- Lagging behind your competition.
- Not prepared to compete in the future.
- Too slow to execute.
- Quick to react, but slow to create, strategize, and plan.
- Too slow to innovate or ineffective innovation.
- Too siloed to collaborate across your business.

> *"If you don't like something, change it.*
> *If you can't change it, change your attitude."*
> Maya Angelou

When you have finished implementing any change in your business, make sure you do **Lessons Learned**.

As you're navigating your business through a change transformation, keep your eyes on your goals and focus on the outcomes you want to achieve. Make decisions and take the necessary actions to focus your business on moving forward. Never say never, tell yourself, when.

This is a favourite saying in my home and my business:

> *"Problems are only solutions looking to be found*
> *– have faith they will be found,*
> *just some take a little longer to find than others."*
> Laurie K. Grant

Next I want to show you what happens to your time. See you in the next chapter. It's all about **Time**.

CHAPTER 3

NOT ENOUGH TIME

ឧឌឈឈឈឧឌឈឈឈ

How Do You Spend Your Time?

When you waste your money, there are opportunities to make more money, but when you waste your time, you cannot get your time back once it's gone. Spending time thinking about the past is crazy; the past is done, it's finished, over, done with, and you cannot change whatever happened there, you only learn from it. The future is a period of time over which you have no control. There is absolutely no point in thinking about what might happen in the future.

Present time is the **ONLY time** over which you have **total control**. The longer your present time exists, the more money you make as you have more control.

Where are you in managing your time – do you see yourself doing any of these? Do you:

- ☐ Give control over your time to everyone else?
- ☐ Get distracted and repeat the same activity over and over?
- ☐ Never have enough time to do everything you want to do?
- ☐ Believe it takes more time to teach someone else to do a task?
- ☐ Have poorly planned and zero-result meetings?
- ☐ Never schedule free time for yourself or enjoy your life?
- ☐ Spend your time on every priority, except your own?
- ☐ Dislike spending your time on creating, visioning, or planning?
- ☐ Believe there is never enough time?

Do you like to spend your time on activities that are your priority for your business in an effective and efficient manner? Are you spending your time on the right activities for you and your business every day? We often misunderstand how we're spending our time, which leads to misplaced productivity or unnoticed practices.

The first step in being in control of your time is understanding what you spend your time on. On the next page is an **Activity Tracking by Hour Worksheet**™ to help you track what activities you spend your time on. I have created it for a Monday to Friday work week; however, feel free to change the days to match your work week. Set an alarm to go off every hour and document how you spent your time for that hour.

I like to use the diagram below to help my clients become aware of the choices they make. Being aware of what you do means you make different choices so you're in control of how you spend your time. With this knowledge, you now spend your time on what matters to you, what you control, and what is aligned with your highest values. This eliminates worrying about what doesn't matter to you, what you cannot control, and what is not aligned with your highest values.

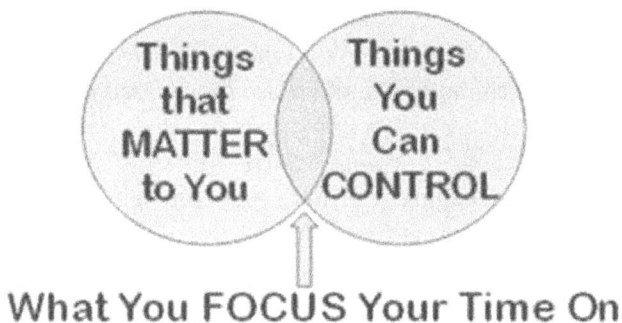

Figure 5 - What You Focus Your Time On

Activity Tracking By Hour

Monday		Tuesday		Wednesday		Thursday		Friday	
Hour	Activity	Hour	Activity	Hour	Activity	Hour	Activity	Hour	Activity
1:00		1:00		1:00		1:00		1:00	
2:00		2:00		2:00		2:00		2:00	
3:00		3:00		3:00		3:00		3:00	
4:00		4:00		4:00		4:00		4:00	
5:00		5:00		5:00		5:00		5:00	
6:00		6:00		6:00		6:00		6:00	
7:00		7:00		7:00		7:00		7:00	
8:00		8:00		8:00		8:00		8:00	
9:00		9:00		9:00		9:00		9:00	
10:00		10:00		10:00		10:00		10:00	
11:00		11:00		11:00		11:00		11:00	
12:00		12:00		12:00		12:00		12:00	
13:00		13:00		13:00		13:00		13:00	
14:00		14:00		14:00		14:00		14:00	
15:00		15:00		15:00		15:00		15:00	
16:00		16:00		16:00		16:00		16:00	
17:00		17:00		17:00		17:00		17:00	
18:00		18:00		18:00		18:00		18:00	
19:00		19:00		19:00		19:00		19:00	
20:00		20:00		20:00		20:00		20:00	
21:00		21:00		21:00		21:00		21:00	
22:00		22:00		22:00		22:00		22:00	
23:00		23:00		23:00		23:00		23:00	
0:00		0:00		0:00		0:00		0:00	

Figure 6 - Activity Tracking by Hour Worksheet^{TM}

Manage Interruptions

With the **Activity Tracking by Hour Worksheet**[TM], you charted your activities over a time period long enough to show you where you spend your time. What is the next step? Look at what you're doing – do you see any patterns? Are you:

- ☐ Planning too many events?
- ☐ Allowing frequent interruptions?
- ☐ Confusing being busy with being effective?
- ☐ Not comfortable with delegating?
- ☐ Saying yes to requests when you wanted to say no?
- ☐ Having a hard time asking for help?
- ☐ Thinking of other things, not what you're currently doing?
- ☐ Spending time worrying about the past or the future?
- ☐ Doing activities that have nothing to do with your business?

Did you know you have to manage interruptions daily, no matter what? Interruptions in your business are costly. Basex in a 2007 study discovered interruptions were costing U.S. businesses $588 billion per year. Imagine how the cost of interruptions increases each year. Imagine what happens when this is repeated over and over. You don't want this for your business, do you?

The problem isn't too much information, although there is lots more information easily available to us now, way more than ever before. The real problem is information is forced into your life, whether you want it or not. Today we have a world of constant interruption. It isn't a question of managing your time, but managing the interruptions, where your attention goes, and what you focus on.

Did you know your mood can be undesirably affected by recurring interruptions? Why? Interruptions prevent you from focusing on your highest priorities. This creates more stress for you. And guess what – you're more unsatisfied and unhappy with your business, giving up on yourself and your great business.

Your interruptions are going to be different depending on what your business does, however every business is affected by a number of common interruptions. They are phone calls, emails, text messages, surfing the internet, people interruptions (clients, employees, and vendors), impromptu meetings, etc.

Minimize interruptions and remove time-wasters from your day, which allows you to accomplish more and become more successful in your business. When you work at recognizing and removing interruptions from your business, this improves the effectiveness of the efforts you put into your business. Do you have any idea what's working and how using your time productively improves your business success? Remember interruptions are found externally in your environment and internally in your mind.

Here are some types of interruptions to be aware of:

- **Complete Interruption** which completely occupies all of your focus and attention.
- **Prevailing Interruption** which occupies most of your focus and attention.
- **Distracted Interruption** doesn't stop you from working, but you begin to slow down or lose accuracy.
- **Background Interruption** diverts part of your attention and you run the risk of slowing down or making errors.

It's important to train yourself to block out interruptions. This is in your best interest. As you practice and evolve this skill, the rewarding results will be to have amazing business success. Let's take a look at self-management skills and what these do for you and your business success.

Learn to Self-manage

Have you found it tough to stay enthused and attentive to your business? What you need to solve these issues is effective self-management and self-motivation skills, which are two of the most important skills for you to learn. Your ability to control your feelings, emotions, and activities is a key skill, which will help you throughout your life. Taking the time to develop self-regulation activities will help you to avoid stress and provide you with more opportunities to get involved in your business success.

"The first and best victory is to conquer self."
Plato

You're accountable for everything that occurs in your business and your life. It's essential for your business success for you to learn to accept complete responsibility for yourself. It's important for you to take control of yourself to direct your life and your business. When you don't take control, other people will take it for you and you may not like how they direct your life or your business. Your life isn't a dress rehearsal; it's the only chance you get. Everything you did or didn't do up until now has created the life you have right now.

When you want to have a different future, you don't wait for the future; it never comes. You make changes in the present time. Who is going to do this? You are. Why, because you want to have a successful business. Learning to self-manage helps you take your brilliant creation into the world. What must you do? You take complete responsibility of yourself, your life and your business to make things change. Why, because things don't change by themselves. If you don't manage yourself, time will manage you.

"We are what we repeatedly do,
excellence then is not an act, but a habit."
Aristotle

Learning to manage yourself halts behaviours that cost you your business, your clients, your employees or your vendors. Learning to delay gratification and snap impulses gives you time to strategize the consequences of the choices or actions you choose. You have a choice in how you react to the situations which occur in your life and your business. When you're self-managed, you:

- Lead with Integrity
- Are Open to Change
- Identify Your Triggers
- Practice Self-discipline
- Are Self-reliant
- Reframe Negative Thoughts
- Keep Calm Under Pressure

- Consider the Consequence
- Believe in Yourself
- Have Values
- Keep Your Word
- Believe in the Good in Others
- Create Good Habits
- Finish What You Start
- Always See Opportunity
- Are Clear in Your Vision, Values, Goal and Priorities
- Express Appropriately
- Accept Feedback
- Are Accountable

I've shown you what it means to be self-managed and the impact it has on your life and your business. Let's now take a look at how your vision, your values, your goals, and your priorities, assist you in having a successful business where you **WOW** your clients, your employees, and your vendors.

Values & Postulates Are Important

Do you know what your highest values are? Do you live and work with them? Well, we're going to talk about values, what they are, why it's important to know them, and to make them a fundamental part of your life and your business. Your values are what you believe is most important in how you live and work.

Your values are fundamental beliefs or guiding principles for your behaviours or actions. Values help you know the difference between right and wrong actions. In business, as well as, in your personal life, values create a steadfast and fixed guide to how you conduct yourself. Values are the compass to keep you on the right path.

> *"When your values are clear to you,*
> *making decisions becomes easier."*
> Roy E. Disney

Values are important and lasting principles or concepts. When commonly shared, values identify what are acceptable and unacceptable actions. When you have a value system, you have an articulated set of values developed and adopted by your business as a standard guide on how all areas of your business perform.

A value statement is a declaration which tells your clients, your employees, and your vendors what your top priorities and beliefs are as a business. This is a great way to remain true to what is important to you in your business and you lead by example. As the fearless leader of your business, you show how your values are important to you.

The core values of your business, support your vision, shape your culture, and identify the essence of your business. These values help you in your decision making, define the quality of your products and/or services, and ensure your clients, your employees, and your vendors know what you as a business stand for. Defining your values, representing them, and keeping them fresh and alive is one of the most vital things you do for your business. Having a core set of values is a competitive advantage in today's marketplace.

> *"Find people who share your values,*
> *and you'll conquer the world together."*
> John Ratzenberger

I know several highly successful businesses who have their core values identified and who review their core values every time three or more of their members meet. Values drive our actions, which create our experiences. When you incorporate values into your business and personal life, you have a compass to guide you creating the ability to provide **WOW** experiences for your clients, your employees, your vendors, and yourself.

Having explicitly stated core values of your business helps:

- Manage relationships with your clients, your employees, and your vendors.
- Direct your business procedures.
- Illuminate who your business is and what it stands for.
- Create accountability for actions, products, decisions, and policy.

- Articulate why you conduct your business the way you do.
- Guide you on how to teach and reward.
- Assist you in making decisions.
- Provide structure for your business.
- Encourage integrity and respect.
- Empower all the people your business interacts with to take initiative and give their best.
- Birth innovative idea with the potential to change the world.

Postulates coupled with your values bring a new way to realize your vision as you won't be limited to the outcomes or the how. A postulate is to have a belief, to make a clear and positive declaration of the outcome you desire, and allow what you believe to be a higher power to bring it forth. You tap into the universal consciousness and all the intelligence contained within it. I've given you an understanding of what values are, why it's important to have them, and to continually share and reinforce them. Next we will look at how your values guide your goals.

Setting Goals & Priorities

What are goals and priorities and why are they important to you and your business? The Business Dictionary describes a goal as *"An observable and measurable end result having one or more objectives to be achieved within a more or less fixed timeframe."* In other words, a goal is an outcome you desire, envision, strategize, and commit to take action on, to achieve by a specific deadline.

The Business Dictionary describes a priority as *"Established right to a certain higher degree, importance, precedence, or rank over others."* In other words, a priority is a task, which is more important than other tasks and has a requirement to be executed or completed first, before any other task.

Goals are powerful resolutions to achieve a desirable result. They give you, your clients, your employees, and your vendors a clear understanding of what your business wants to accomplish. A big goal is easier to reach when you break it down into smaller short-term goals which have reachable milestones. Goals give your business tasks or processes, meaning and provide reasons for your business decisions.

To be a successful business, it's important to set prioritized goals. However, your goals are derived from and aligned with your vision and values. When you don't have your vision and your values, your business has no purpose. Prioritized, strategic goals are part of your business plan and need to be tweaked as required.

You want your business to be profitable. To be profitable, you need to make sales and manage expenses. Your goals then are in meeting your sales targets and keeping track of your expenses – even deferring purchases that aren't really required. Your business needs to improve, innovate, and grow to be more profitable. With quantifiable goals, you measure the success of your business. You might not predict your business future, but you can definitely plan for it.

I like to teach my clients to set goals as it provides them with a solid framework for working on their business. When you have set business goals, you choose activities or tasks that help you to achieve your business goals instead of doing those that won't help you. You need to show by example, so everyone knows to work on activities and tasks to support your business.

You have greater confidence in making your business decisions when you have clearly defined and stated business goals. Goals need to be documented. A good goal statement is specific, positive, and realistic. Having transparency of your business goals drives your business performance. Having strategic business goals aids in your decision-making as you have a better understanding of the implications of the decision. Goals need to be updated as they are met and/or changed to meet the needs of your business.

Here are two ways to set your goals – **S.M.A.R.T.** and **C.L.E.A.R.**

S.M.A.R.T

- **Specific** – Don't be vague, make it simple and easily understood by everyone.
- **Measurable** – A goal must be tracked and measured to know when it's achieving the desired outcome.

- **Attainable** – A goal needs to be achievable – sometimes it's good to have 3 levels – easy to accomplish, needs to be accomplished or beyond your wildest dreams accomplished.
- **Realistic** – A goal needs to have the resources, knowledge and time to obtain it.
- **Timely** – A goal needs a fixed timeframe.

C.L.E.A.R.

- **Collaborative** – Encourage participants to work together.
- **Limited** – Manage by limiting scope and time.
- **Emotional** – Tap into the participants' passion.
- **Appreciable** – Break into smaller chunks for quick achievement.
- **Refinable** – Adapt to change, tweak as required.

Some questions to ask when setting your goals and your priorities are:

- What needs to be achieved?
- What are the pros and cons?
- Are there any alternatives?
- With whom?

- Where?
- How?
- When?
- Why?

Here's a little story about time and goals. One of my client's I worked with had a 24-hour, 365 days a year support team for an online discount stock brokerage. This was a complex system requiring a large knowledge base to support it efficiently.

At 3:00 am in the morning, when a support person has been woken up to handle a trouble call, it's more efficient and timely to have a manual on-hand, but they didn't have one. I created a goal with my client to have a manual for their support team to use on all their calls.

I initiated and supervised the creation of a 150-page manual for this team. It required copious amounts of research from reading documentation and information gathering interviews. This support manual covered a complete system description, including servers and their locations, firewalls, database, vendor feeds, overnight batch transactions, etc. It had a complete list of when to escalate and to whom you escalated. There was a list of known issues and their workarounds. I worked with my client's programmers to automate several standard inquiries to a Sybase database.

This manual not only improved efficiency, it improved the relations my client had with their own clients and with their support team as now the system up-time had been increased significantly. This solution was a win-win for everyone and provided a **WOW** experience for my client, their clients, and their support team.

Let's now look at putting this all together to see what you do to help you manage a clear focus on your business.

Create a Clear Focus

I've taken you through how you spend your time, how you manage yourself and interruptions and what are your vision, your values, your goals, and you. Let's identify ways you create a clear focus for you to move forward in your business. However, before we get into the business things you do, here are some lifestyle choices to aid you in achieving a clear focus.

- Get Enough Sleep
- Move Your Body
- Eat Brain Healthy Nutrient Rich Foods
- Limit Alcohol
- Reduce Stress
- Avoid Distractions
- Exercise Your Brain, Learn New Things
- Meditate, Practice Yoga or Dance
- Find Your Best Time of Day
- Create the Ideal Environment
- Have Consistent Routines
- Practice Meditation and Visualization

I work with my clients to create a strategic plan for how they implement the changes they want to make. Be accountable by making others aware of your strategic plan to help ensure you stay on track.

Take the appropriate action steps you need to put your strategic plan into play. Prioritize your tasks, preferably the night before, so you do the most critical first. Pay attention to your health, get enough sleep, and drink lots of water to keep hydrated.

> *"When it is obvious that the goals cannot be reached,*
> *don't adjust the goals, adjust the action steps."*
> Confucius

Laser Focus Time Activity™
Ok, you're ready to focus, but you don't know how to begin. Here's a way I teach my clients. Start small by making a decision to focus on one activity to the exclusion of all else for 1 minute. Set a timer. Give yourself a 1-minute reward; something that's fun, feels good, and lets you know you succeeded. Do this again and again for at least 15-20 times during your work day. See how much you get accomplished.

Do this for 5 days increasing your focus time for 1 minute every day while keeping the reward to 1 minute. On the 6th day increase the reward time to 2 minutes. Continue to increase your focus time by 1 minute every day. On the 11th day increase the reward time to 3 minutes. Continue to increase your focus time by 1 minute every day. On the 16th day increase the reward time to 4 minutes.

Continue to increase your focus time by 1 minute every day. On the 21st day increase the reward time to 5 minutes. Continue to increase your focus time by 1 minute until you're able to focus for 25 minutes with a 5-minute reward. You can leave it like this or you carry on with the same pattern until you focus for 50 minutes with a 10-minute reward. You will be amazed at what you accomplish when you are laser focused.

Focus Time	1	2	3	4	5	6	7	8	9	10	11	12	13	14	15	16	17	18	19	20	21	22	23	24	25
Reward Time	1	1	1	1	1	2	2	2	2	2	3	3	3	3	3	4	4	4	4	4	5	5	5	5	5

Figure 7 - Laser Focus Time Chart™

This is all fine and dandy, you've learned how to focus, but you also want to pay attention to what you're going to focus on. How do you do this? Remember, when I talked about your goals and your priorities – guess what – this is your focus list.

When both your short and long-term goals are prioritized, and aligned with your vision and values, then you create achievable to-do lists (I do mine at the end of the work day for the next day). Make appointments in your calendar with deadlines. To stay focused, remember to avoid distractions, reduce stress, set achievable goals, have downtime, and don't forget to reward yourself.

I like to reflect at the end of my work day on what went well and what didn't so I make adjustments in how I am the next day. I create my to-do list for the next day at this time. I shut off the phones and the computer to have a calm sanctuary where I focus on my reflecting. While I'm reflecting, I visualise how it looks and feels when I nail my goals. Visualising future victories creates momentum and drive to succeed. I also create a to-don't-do list, which helps me focus on unproductive habits I want to change.

Next, let's look at your **Environment**, where you work and what it looks like, as this all plays a factor in how well you work, what kind of successes you have and your overall sense of well-being.

CHAPTER 4

WHERE'S YOUR DESK?

What is Your Business Environment?

What is your business environment and why is it important to you in conducting your business? Your business environment is the place where you spend the majority of your time executing your business, whether it's in an office in your home, a warehouse, a factory, an office building or on the road visiting your clients either locally or out-of- town with a hotel room as your base.

A chaotic business environment hampers your business proficiency. Do you want to have your business fail because you created an environment that wasn't aligned with your business vision? Go back to your vision and your values for your business and extend those to the environment you and your employees work in, and where you interact with your clients and your vendors.

Your business environment is the complete set of inside and outside influences affecting the outcomes of your business. These inside and outside elements influence each other and work together to affect a business. Remember, nothing exists in a vacuum, so all the people, resources, places, and regulations create your business environment and influence the progress, performance and results of your business.

What does a well-structured, systemized, efficient workplace do for you? It fosters innovative collaboration, reduces stress, encourages productivity, and ultimately generates more business. This is vital for your business to thrive year after year after year. Your business success will grow in leaps and bounds when you do this. It improves your morale and the morale of everyone involved in your business.

You believe your business environment is just about what your workspace looks like, but it's much more than that. It's about mindset, mood, health, safety, and energy. You attract like-minded clients, employees, and vendors. People know you're a professional who's invested in their success, you demonstrate a commitment to your business and that your business takes pride in a job well done.

As you see from the diagrams, different external and internal factors have a direct impact on your business environment. It's important you understand these factors and how to adapt to them as they arise and, trust me, they will. It's an inevitable part of having a business, no matter how big or small.

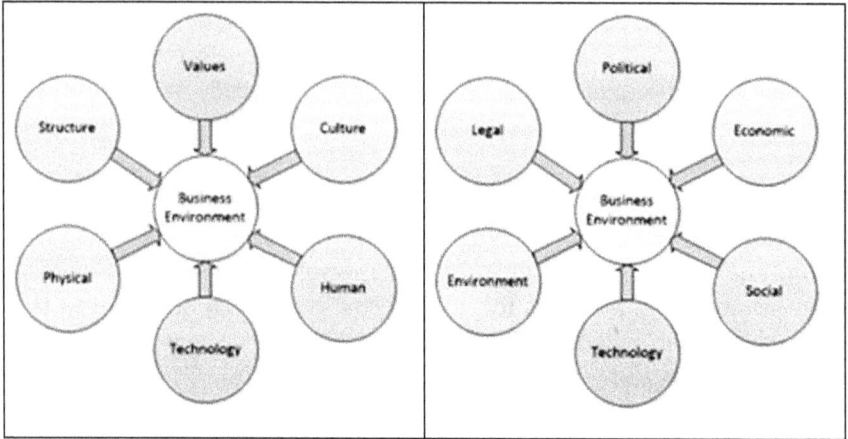

Figure 8 – Inside Environment Influences **Figure 9 - Outside Environment Influences**

Why is it important to understand your business environment? It's important because there's a direct relationship between your business environment and how well your business performs in the marketplace. Many factors affect your business environment and have a great impact on your survival and growth. Understanding these influences enables you to:

Know Your Prospects and Pressures so you rise to meet the challenges you encounter in the workplace.

Give Instructions for Business Growth which allows you to look at new areas for business development.

Achieve Constant Knowledge as you and your business personnel are motivated to continually learn new knowledge and skills to meet the changes in your industry.

Identify Your Business Strengths and Weaknesses which helps you to chart your business course of action to survive in your industry.

Know Your Business Competition as this helps you examine your competitors' strategies and articulate your own business strategies to be competitive in your industry.

Inside Environment Influences

Structural Influences are about how your business is organized, and the management styles you use, which are all factors to influence your business decisions.

Value Influences are taken from what you as the conductor of your business determine are important. These are found in your mission, your vision, your values, your goals, your policies, and your practices. How successfully you share these throughout your business is a contributing factor to your business success.

Cultural Influences are usually driven from the top down. It's important to know what your vision, your values, your goals, and your priorities are for your business as this influences your business policy, the systems you put in place, the language you use, and your overall business environment. You want to influence the shared culture in your business as it's an important feature that enhances your business success greatly.

Human Influences are things like the skills, commitment, talent, and attitudes of your employees, which factor into how your business performs. The participation and resourcefulness of your employees depend on your business culture. You're the one to set the standard. Look at how you develop your human resources, as well as, the procedures and interactions between them and in your business. This improves the usefulness and competence of your business overall.

Physical Influences are the physical aspects of your business and what kind of state they are in. When you aren't vigilant in watching this influence, it has an adverse effect on your business success.

Technology Influences are something you need to monitor as staying abreast of the changes in technology is key to making all the difference as to how well you succeed in the marketplace.

Outside Environment Influences

A **PESTEL** analysis is a means to analyse and understand the outside environment influences that impact your business. You use the results from a **PESTEL** analysis in a **PACT**[TM] analysis. Below are the parts of a **PESTEL**:

Political Influences are:
- Tax Policy
- Foreign Trade Policy
- Laws Governing Business
- Business Regulations
- Government Stability
- Social Policy
- Health and Safety Requirements

Economic Influences are:
- Taxes
- Inflation
- Interest and Exchange Rates
- Wages
- Credit
- Buyers Income

Social Influences are:
- Population Dynamics
- Wealth Distribution
- Lifestyle Trends and Changes
- Educational and Career Trends
- Cultural Expectations
- Income Statistics

Technology Influences are:
- New Technology
- Technology Change Rates
- Technology Obsolescence Rates
- New Goods / Services Production / Distribution
- New Target Market Communication
- Technology Legislation

Environment Influences are:
- Raw Material Availability
- Natural Disasters
- Transportation Access
- Carbon Footprint Targets
- Waste Disposal
- Environmental Protection

Legal Influences are:
- Employment
- Health and Safety
- Products
- Advertising
- Patents
- Consumers

Clear Your Business Clutter

Business clutter comes in many shapes and forms. You need to understand what business clutter is and the ways you manage it before it manages you and sends your business into a downward spiral. Business clutter weakens efficiency and incentive.

When you have business **CALM**, you have a structure; and clear and easy to follow process, policy, and procedures. This structure gives all the people involved with your business a great mindset and motivation to work with your business. When you're committed to having a **CALM** business, you define what areas of your business benefit by decluttering.

Decide your goals and schedule your business decluttering by booking appointments in your calendar. Make business decluttering a planned activity. Streamlining your business brings you, your clients, your employees and your vendors peace of mind – business **CALM**.

There are several types of clutter you find creeping around in your business. To **WOW** your clients, your employees, your vendors and yourself, it's a wise idea to be mindful and watch out for these.

Keep in mind, **Less is More** so it's important to look for ways to simplify your business to provide **WOW** experiences for your clients, your employees, your vendors and yourself.

Physical clutter is the easiest to identify because you see it. Look around your business, no matter where it's located, and what do you see? Is there a mess of papers to be filed, or sticky notes everywhere to remind you or piles of books or file folders or business cards or leftover dishes or food that require your attention? Then it's time for you to schedule a clean-up. I've been a consultant in a variety of companies where there was a clean desk policy and you had to not only clear your desk every night, but you had to turn your papers over whenever anyone came to speak with you.

The price of **virtual clutter** is astonishingly high because virtual clutter is usually not noticed. If you're like most people, you're too busy to notice the various types of virtual clutter you find on your computer and stored on your servers. How might you avoid some of this clutter? Do you review the materials you keep electronically to see if you still require them? Are they're outdated; do they need to be updated or archived or even deleted?

Product clutter is the most universally recognized form of clutter. Have you ever thought having many products creates needless pressure on you and your business? Excessive product inventory decreases the real significance in the client's mind. Everyone is busy: your potential clients don't have time to sift through your product clutter to figure out what they want to buy. Your inventory has become common place and unexceptional. Clients aren't working with you because of your product inventory; they work with you because they trust you, they believe in you and your capabilities. Remember the **Less is More** rule and **WOW** your clients, your employees and your vendors.

Client clutter happens when you have clients that have a negative emotional effect because of their behaviour. Why do you do this? You've decided your client and their money is more important than your business, your vision, your values, or your employees. Yes, there are days when your clients are difficult; you learn methods to cope, but when you're continually disrespected, it's time to re-evaluate your position and release your toxic client without any regret.

Another type of clutter to look at is **emotional clutter**. Emotional clutter is way more problematic because there is no visual element. Emotional clutter is baggage related to undesirable attitudes and belief systems. Emotional clutter likes to dress up as something for your good and pretends it does you no harm. Is emotional clutter spoiling your business success? We've talked about the benefits of cleaning up your business clutter. Guess what, there's a great benefit to you in clearing out old pains and traumas. The toxic patterns created by emotional clutter prevents you from having the business of your dreams.

Develop a Business Mindset

Let's talk about what makes a good business mindset, which is one of the most important pieces to having a successful business. Before you work on developing a successful business, you want to make sure you have a business mindset. What does this mean, you ask? A business mindset is your habits, your beliefs, your passions, and your attitudes. When you have a growth mindset, you expand what you know; you learn new skills and overcome obstacles.

When you have a business mindset you're in the pursuit of making money by serving your clients. For success in your business, you need to be mentally resilient. Developing a business mindset gives you a compass to steer your business on the way to success. How do you do this, you ask? Guess what, I'm going to share this with you.

Believe in Yourself – Have a positive attitude to create your route to success. When you believe in yourself, others do too. This is how you create the flexibility and determination needed when times get difficult. Believe in your dreams; believe in your heart of hearts you can do it and you will do it.

Do What You Love – Follow your passion and you will want to work your business, to nurture and grow your business and be committed to serving your clients, your employees, and your vendors.

Think for Yourself – Don't let other people do your thinking for you. It's your business. Yes, it's helpful to look at what people are saying, but the ultimate decision must rest with you or it will nag at you forever.

Be Strategic – Make sure the end result you want aligns with your vision, your values, your goals, and your priorities.

Be Open to Continually Learning – When you have knowledge, you have power, you're more confident, and you're prepared to move your business forward; therefore, continue to research, read, question, and listen.

Know Your Purpose – What is the purpose of your business? To serve your clients and make money. Make your vision, your values, your goals, and your priorities visual; have dates for their achievement.

Know Your Profitability – What are your sales goals, your competitive advantage, your cash flow, and your tactical profit indicators?

Know Your Strategy – Look at all the parts of your business, look ahead, plan for your vision, your values, your goals, your priorities, and turn your challenges into opportunities.

Be Courageous – Push yourself to go beyond your comfort zone, at the very least you grow and learn. There are no easy routes up the mountain of success, you must meet many obstacles along the way. What matters is how you face these challenges. Look at each challenge as an opportunity to learn and grow. Take risks, face rejection and failure – you learn from them.

Hire Great People – Create a supportive A-team comprised of motivated, successful, goal-minded people. Surround yourself with people who tell you the truth and support you.

Be Selective – Look at everything from many angles. Pay attention to things like who does the best job, which client moves you forward, and be open to changing in an instant.

And, Last, but not Least...

Be Grateful – Practice the art of gratitude, be thankful for every experience, express your gratitude for every success and every challenge or obstacle; they all teach you. When you are grateful, you attract success to you. Your customers are more loyal, your employees are more productive and committed and your vendors are more supportive when you are grateful for what they do for you and your business.

Embrace Change

We talked about change early on to understand what change is, why it's difficult, fear of it, types of change, change models and change management, but to be effective in your business environment you need to know how to cope with change. Change is one of the few constants in life. You need to learn to embrace and endorse changes in your business.

One of the best ways to manage change is to see it as a system, a process with various steps to it. You need to reframe your thinking about change. You and your business will thrive despite change. Change for most people isn't easy, it's downright uncomfortable. However, you're going to learn ways to confront change, to let you be in charge, and for you to be in the driver's seat.

"Most of the important things in the world have been
accomplished by people who have kept on trying when
there seemed to be no hope at all."
Dale Carnegie

Start by breathing. Count to ten if you must. Then dive in, embrace the change, and watch as you and your business successfully come out the other side. The most important first step to manage change is to understand it. Most people are afraid of change because it takes them into the unknown. However, when you embrace change and look at change as an adventure, it is now a way to stretch yourself and your business and to learn and grow. Face your fears, knowing change is an opportunity for growth.

You need to be prepared for change as you never know when change comes or what shape change comes in. It's best to take the appropriate steps to prepare. Learn as much about the changing situation so you know what you can control and how much control you have over the change.

I teach these useful strategies to help you, when change arrives, to be flexible and to be part of the change. Adopt an attitude of eagerness and enthusiasm. Welcome change as an opportunity to examine your business. Be an influencer and a driver of change in your business. Apply wisdom from past experiences. Communication is important. Talk with others who have similar experiences. You never know what you will learn to use in your situation. Focus on the issue, develop a plan of action, and ask for advice. Look for all the positives to keep you afloat while you steer your business through the waters of change.

When change is beyond your control, accept the change, relax, and go with the change. Trying to resist is futile; change happens anyway. It's better to go along for the ride and view change as an opportunity to learn and grow. Don't bother blaming or complaining; it isn't going to make any difference. Blaming and complaining will just add to your stress. You're not an effective champion of your business when you're stressed out. You, the fearless leader of your business, need to set the example.

Learn to let go and look forward, not backward. No sense in wasting time wishing for change not to occur. It will anyway. Don't focus on the past, look to the future and embrace change.

"Markets change, tastes change, so the companies and the individuals who choose to compete in those markets must change."
An Wang

One of the ways to manage change in your business is to break the change down into smaller chunks of planned effort called **Programs** and **Projects.** Let's take a look at why you have projects and how they help you accomplish change in an effective way in your business.

CHAPTER 5

PROGRAMS & PROJECTS

ೞಙಖಖಲೞಙಖಖಲ

How to Get from Here to There

Hello there, glad to see you're still with me on the **Systemization** journey. We've looked at Business Chaos, Business Calm, Change, Time, and Environment. I want to explore how you execute your work, whether it be day-to-day tasks or a one-time initiative.

The first thing you must know is where your starting and ending points are and what is in between. Guess what, there's a great strategic tool for this – a **GAP** Analysis.

What is a **GAP** Analysis? In simple terms, it's where your business is currently, where you want your business to be in the future and what's missing or what you have to do to get your business there. Whenever you want to change something in your business, it's a useful tool to help you decide what you need to do to achieve your desired future state. It assists you in identifying activities you need to complete to get the results you want. A **GAP** analysis makes you look at what you're doing in your business; how well your business is functioning and performing.

I help my clients analyse this report to create specific programs and/or projects to move their business towards the future state they want. The important thing to remember here is you're aligning with your vision, your values, your goals, and your priorities.

Another great tool I use to get from here to there is a **PACT**™ analysis, which helps you look at where your business is internally – your **Prospects** and your **Assets** and where your business is externally – your **Challenges** and your **Threats**. What makes this tool particularly powerful is it assists you to uncover business opportunities you're positioned to achieve. Plus, when you know the liabilities in your business, you're able to remove them or at the very least, manage them so they don't take you by surprise. You apply this tool against your business or a product and/or a service.

You can change your internal factors such as your business reputation, your products and/or services, or your business location, but you have to adapt to the external factors your business encounters, which are your competitors, your vendors, or your pricing for your products and/or services.

I like to use a **PACT**™ analysis to help my clients create business strategies as the results help to differentiate them from their competition, which in turn allows them to compete successfully. When you're a new business, I use a **PACT**™ analysis as part of your planning as there is no one size fits all. It's important to see your new business from its unique perspective to start on the right path for your business. This saves you from a lot of challenges, headaches, and heartache as your business starts to grow. When you're an already existing business, a **PACT**™ analysis is helpful whenever you want to innovate or there is a change in the marketplace. It's a good idea to do a **PACT**™ analysis at least once a year as part of your overall business review and planning.

There are two more factors to look at; one is what are your **Core Business Competencies** and the other is what is your **USP** or **Unique Selling Proposition**.

Core Business Competencies are what allows your business to compete. Once you know what your core competencies are, direct your business focus on what it does best and when necessary outsource. This allows you to cultivate your business capability in areas of importance to your clients.

This, coupled with your **USP,** allows you to identify your competitive edge – what your business offers that your competition doesn't. This helps you to target your business improvements and your sales efforts. You need to ensure these are important to your clients. Make sure the marketplace, knows what your core competencies and your USP are. Don't be surprised when your competitors work to knock you down.

Plan Smaller Chunks of Work

You've decided on some activities you want to do in your business to meet your vision, your values, your goals, and your priorities. How are you going to tackle this work? This is where programs and projects help.

Program Management is a high-level method to help you manage a large change in your business or when you're establishing new processes or improvements to existing processes. You group like-minded projects to deliver specific pieces of functionality to work in collaboration to achieve positive and common outcomes. Programs are used when you're making essential business changes that require expenditures, which have significant business impact on your finances like revenue and costs. Programs are for long term strategic plans that are tied to what's going on in the marketplace and your vision, your values, your goals, and your priorities.

Program Management concentrates on integration and communications. Program Management has control over the program's resources and priorities. In summary, Program Management addresses the management of a portfolio of projects, creating and establishing your project processes, monitoring and measuring your project results, and coordinating related projects.

Project Management is the method used to deliver a project, which adheres to established processes. A project provides you the ability to create plans to manage, control and deploy key milestones, deliverables, and resources from start to finish. Projects are sequentially organized activities with a defined start and end, deliverables and outcomes, planned schedules, and budgets with assigned resources.

Projects are not your normal business operations; they are unique with a specific objective. Managing your projects effectively gives you a great opportunity to achieve your desired results, provide the best use of your resources and satisfy the varying requirements of your stakeholders.

Projects have a few core phases as follows:

- **Conception/Initiation** – Get the business case for the project, the approvals, and the finances in place.
- **Definition/Planning** – Create a plan, a charter, work scope, the budget, and define required resources.
- **Launch/Execution** – Perform the project work.
- **Project Performance/Control** – Track against plan and adjust as necessary.
- **Project Close** – Validate the project met the objectives, the client approves, and conduct the lessons learned.

When you break a large piece of work down into smaller pieces of work, you want to ensure the work is a stand-alone module with a clear purpose and defined inputs, outputs, start and end. This makes the work less intimidating and more manageable.

> *"Do what you can, with what you have, where you are."*
> Theodore Roosevelt

Some ways to help with breaking work down:

- Look at the big picture and understand what your desired end result is.
- Look at the different pieces of the work.
- Decide on the steps to take.
- Put your steps into a logical order – what is 1st, 2nd, 3rd, etc.
- Generate a timeline with a deadline for completion.
- Have a plan to stay on track and stick with it.
- Schedule a final review at the end.

Hire for Specific Tasks

You've created your program and/or projects, you've planned the work, and now you need to acquire the employees to complete the work. You may or may not have the requisite skills in your business to complete the work. What you need is a **Staffing Plan** and then to execute the plan.

What is a **Staffing Plan**, you might ask? A **Staffing Plan** identifies the skill sets you need, where you're going to find the people with those skills, and what is your selection and on-boarding process. It's a good idea to consider other resources like tools, equipment, software, etc. This is one of the most important pieces of getting your project completed successfully.

> *"Never hire someone who knows less than you*
> *do about what he's hired to do."*
> Malcolm Forbes

You consider existing employees if they have the right skills, but then you're taking them away from other important work you require them to do. The trend these days is to hire contractors so you have employees directly dedicated to your project. But before you dive into this activity, you need to understand the project's purpose and be very clear on your desired objectives for your end results.

I encourage my clients to use a template to create their **Staffing Plan**. Why? It makes sure you don't forget an important piece of your plan, you save time, they provide consistency and are reusable. In your **Staffing Plan,** you want to identify your project team's responsibilities for meetings, reporting, communication, authority, control, and project activities.

Have contingencies in your **Staffing Plan** for replacing employees because they are ill or they quit or any other reason which presents a risk to the timely completion of your project. Ensure your project's human resources (HR) practices are aligned with your already established HR rules, policies, and practices. Monitor your **Staffing Plan** throughout your project's life to ensure your **Staffing Plan** remains pertinent.

Points to consider in your **Staffing Plan**:

- What kind of skill sets are required?
- How do you obtain the employee?
- How long do you want the employee for?
- What training does the employee need?
- How do you train your employee?
- What is your project's timeline?
- What is the available budget for staffing your project?

> *"I hire people brighter than me and*
> *then I get out of their way."*
> Lee Iacocca

Remember, you want to build a strong team. Consider the dynamics of your team and what strengths they bring to your project. You want each person's skills to balance or complement the other skills on your team.

Make sure everyone knows how they contribute to your project and to your vision, your values, your goals, and your priorities. It's important to create an atmosphere of inclusion for your project employees with your regular business employees.

Project Team Hiring Activities

- Define Project Roles
- Candidate Interviews
- Candidate Selection
- Candidate Search
- Candidate Testing
- On boarding

Project Execution

Project execution is the longest phase of your project lifecycle; it usually takes the greatest energy and the greatest resources. This is where you need to monitor and control your project. You need to implement a variety of management processes to help you in this project phase:

Time	Cost	Quality	Change	Risk
Issues	Procurement	Communications	Checkpoints	Acceptance

Your project is ready to get underway – how are you going start and complete your project?

How about a **Kickoff Meeting**? This is a ½ to 1 full day meeting to:

- Obtain project buy-in.
- Provide a project overview.
- Describe individual roles.
- Build team synergy.
- Review project goals and project deliverables.
- Communicate project timelines, project milestones, and project checkpoints.
- Share the project communications, change management, and reporting structure.

You need to ensure everyone on your project is performing quality work conforming to the project's requirements and meeting applicable standards and guidelines. The project team needs to have work assigned, the results reviewed, and their problems resolved. Where needed, provide training and mentoring to improve skill sets. Allow your project team to easily share information across your project. Get weekly project status reports to inform you of what was completed, what is coming next, what are the current milestones and deliverables, and any issues and/or risks. Have project status meetings to discuss the information you get in the status reports across your project team. Have a change management process in place to effectively manage scope creep. Capture all variances to plans and schedules. Provide regular communication updates to all your project stakeholders. Address all issues and risks in a timely fashion.

Your project team members must pay attention to their due dates and their deliverables. In managing the work being done, you work with four key parts:

- **Who is Doing What Work and by When** – The project activities and the project employee.
- **What Affects their Work** – The issues and risks which are occurring.
- **Who is Depending on the Deliverables** – The internal and external dependencies.
- **Who Needs to Know What** – The timely communication with all required parties.

Bear in mind not everything in your project will go as planned. There are many reasons why things go sideways. You need to have contingency plans in place to manage this. It's important to be prepared to manage change as there undoubtedly will be requirements for change as your project progresses. These come from both internal and external sources, such as organizational, technical, environmental, and end user. At the end of this phase, conduct a checkpoint to confirm your project met its purpose as planned.

Measurable Outcomes

Why do you want to measure the outcomes or results of your project? You want to see how successful you were meeting your desired objectives and if your project is providing a return on your investment.

Sometimes you won't see the return on investment until much later, after your project completion.

You need to have a way of knowing your project is on the right track so setting specific, measurable outcomes help to ensure you're on target. It's important to spend the time to have a clear understanding of your project objectives, the strategies you use to meet those objectives, and the criteria you evaluate your project's progress against.

Many projects fail because they don't have clearly detailed, measurable objectives. Your objectives focus on what your project achieves, not what it produces. I advise my clients to have a specific and well defined target of why they're doing this project. This helps you to know when your objective is successfully achieved. You achieve your objectives when you do this. With clear objectives, you're able to apply the appropriate strategies to meet them. When you have the means to measure your project's progress, then you have the opportunity to make corrections as required. The outcomes need to be specific, measurable, and meaningful.

These are the elements I advise my clients to include in their project objectives:

- A brief and clear description of your objective.
- How you will measure the outcome of your objective.
- Use plain language – no technical gobbledygook, abbreviations or acronyms.
- Make sure it aligns with your vision, your values, your goals, and your priorities.
- Have key milestones to check on your progress in meeting your objective.
- Start the description with a verb e.g. increase, expand, improve.
- Make sure you capture the who, the what, and the how.
- Write your objective as a change statement – (does it decrease, stay the same or increase).

Outcomes need to be specific, measurable, and meaningful in fulfilling a purpose. Outcomes are changes in performance. Outcomes aren't activities or a process such as conducting workshops or developing new protocols. Those aren't outcomes, they're outputs. They don't reflect achieved results and don't prove the worth of your project; instead they're tasks to support your outcomes. The long-term benefits or changes you seek from doing your project are your outcomes.

You know what your objectives are and what outcomes you want; what are outputs? They are the practices, services or products you need to meet the outcomes. They may be brand new, or they may be fixes, or adaptations of things you already have in your business. Now you have the tools to create your progress.

This example puts it all together for you.

OBJECTIVES	OUTCOMES	OUTPUTS
To implement an effective and efficient process for the collection of money from clients.	Strengthened integrity of the financial process through better management of the client monetary collection process.	A new process to bill clients 50% at the start of engagement, 25% at the half-way point, and 25% after final sign off.
	Reduction in the total value and number of payments which cannot be collected from a client.	
	Reduction in the number of invoices incorrectly issued for clients who have already paid.	
	More efficient and earlier collection of client monies.	

Lessons Learned

Ok, your project is finished and you believe it went alright even though it had a few twists and turns along the way. One of the most important things you do at the end of your project is a review, or what is commonly known as **Lessons Learned**.

What you glean from this is valuable information you need to retain and implement in your next projects. The lesson learned might be a new process or a better way of handing a process, or an outcome you want to repeat, or something you don't want to repeat. Basically, you want to know what worked well or what didn't work well.

> *"Begin at the beginning,' the King said gravely,*
> *'and go on till you come to the end; then stop."*
> Lewis Carroll, Alice in Wonderland

Lessons Learned are categorized as:

- What were the positive situations you want to repeat?
- What were any unpleasant situations you want to avoid?

I encourage my clients to do **Lessons Learned** as it's a great way for your business to benefit, and to find ways to improve the performance and efficiency of your projects. You cannot assume the new knowledge just shows up in your next project, you must make a process for this to happen.

How do you perform your **Lessons Learned**? Glad you asked. You schedule a review meeting with at least your project manager and your project owners. It's a good idea as part of your project plan to have **Lessons Learned** documented as they occur during the project. Capturing the **Lessons Learned** during the project helps to ensure the lesson is documented accurately.

Some recommended project areas to cover in your **Lessons Learned** are:

Project Management	People/Roles	Vendor Management
Project Planning	Project Communication	Training
Change Control	Testing/QA	Deployment
Requirements	Architecture/Technical Solution	Transition to Operations

You need to know how to document your **Lessons Learned** so they serve you as a tool in your projects going forward. Your **Lessons Learned** are important for retaining knowledge, reducing risks, and improving the performance of your projects.

Keep your **Lessons Learned** as part of your business assets with your other project documents and in their own **Lessons Learned** database. Make your **Lessons Learned** available for all your projects going forward. A good way to do this is to:

- Identify when the situation occurred in the project.
- Describe the 6Ws: **Who, What, Where, When, Why, and How**.
- Provide the solutions or recommendations.

The **Yellow School Bus** is a great example of **Lessons Learned**. What is a **Yellow School Bus**? They are special distinctive yellow buses used in Toronto to take children who require special schooling to programs in schools not in their regular school district. The company decided one summer they wanted to automate the bus scheduling for the pick-up and drop-off of the children. They didn't want to do the scheduling manually by map anymore.

All summer I worked with the programmer developing the software for this automated scheduling. School starts the day after Labour Day. The week before all the information about the children, their schools, the pick-up and drop-off times, and the addresses had been fed into the program. The reports were run and the schedules made. Off went the yellow school buses to take the children where they needed to go.

But wait, something isn't quite right. Slowly the phones started to ring and increased by the minute until the operators were no longer able to handle all the calls. What was going on? **Chaos. Sheer Chaos** was happening as children didn't get picked-up either from home or from school, or they were picked-up and they were delivered to the wrong place. The company had let the manual scheduling system go. They only relied on the automated system.

We spent the next three days around the clock in the big war room, manually scheduling all the children. The programmer and I had to iron all the bugs out of the automated system and then run it in parallel with the manual scheduling system for at least one month to ensure the scheduling worked correctly.

What are the **Lessons Learned** from this experience? It's the importance of never letting go of a system until you know the new system works; it's better to run both in parallel. This includes changing a manual system to another manual system, a manual system to an automated system or changes to an already existing automated system.

To recap, in this chapter on Programs and Projects, I covered how to get from here to there with a few tools such as a **GAP** and a **PACT**[TM] analysis, plus your core competencies and your unique selling proposition. I explored projects and programs, how to hire for your projects, how to execute your projects, what are objectives, outcomes and outputs, and finally, capturing **Lessons Learned**.

Next I want to take you on a journey through your **Business Data** or your business information and look at what is business data, what business data you capture, how your business data helps you be innovative and how to provide those empowering experiences to **WOW** your clients, your employees, and your vendors.

CHAPTER 6

CAPTURE YOUR BUSINESS DATA

ŒŊŊŊŒŊŊŊ

Take Control of Your Business Data

Your business is up and running, you have your vision, you're serving and **WOW**ing your clients, your employees, and your vendors. But wait, what are you doing with all your valuable business information or data? In today's world, your business is online and connected. One of your challenges is your capability to take control of your business data, to eliminate inefficiencies, especially as you grow your business. Global research states growing sales and reducing operating costs are the greatest business priorities no matter what industry you're in, how you conduct your business or where you're located in the world today.

In business, today, it's mandatory you comprehend an ever-increasing quantity of business, marketplace, and social data to drive effective business decisions to stay competitive. Many new business intelligence and analytics solutions are entering the market place which requires new data systems or training your employees on new tools. How do you handle this?

You need to control your business data. One of the first things I do to help my clients start building their business data model is to look at their business data. You want to find out what data you capture, how you capture it, how long you keep your data, how you store your data, who you share your data with, how you protect your data's privacy, what is the lifespan of your data, how you dispose of your data, what data you need to keep to satisfy the laws of where you conduct your business, etc. The right solutions not only help you solve your business data challenges, they also provide the processes and structures to model your business data.

"Through 2016, 25% of organizations using consumer data
will face reputation damage due to inadequate
understanding of information trust issues."
Doug Laney, Gartner

When you get your business model correct, you will comprehend how data is used by your business, how to manage compliance and risk, and to confidently drive your business forward. Be aware while your business information is considered a valuable asset, collecting too much unfocused data can quickly lose its value and become a business liability. In our current economic climate, cost is a major factor affecting your business operations and service delivery. You must be vigilant and continually be looking for effective means to reduce your business operating costs.

> *"Many data governance organizations struggle to obtain executive sponsorship, in part because they have not linked data quality to improve business performance."*
> Tom Mongoven, Deloitte Consulting LLP

Taking control of your business data means having a business data model, a data strategy, and a data plan. The quality of your data is important. What is the right data for you to capture? Each data type has different standards. There's no point in spending countless hours fixing address data if you never mail your clients because all your client interactions are through email or Skype or some other online communication tool.

How do you ensure you're not included in the many businesses that fail because of poor data management? You need to safeguard your data, making it correct and dependable to support your key business objectives. Data governance must be a long-term objective for your business. When you manage your data efficiently, you improve your bottom line.

The many types of data you collect are influenced by the changing aspects of business, technology, security, privacy, and compliance needs. You need to know where your data lives, who can access it, what they do with your data, and if your data is secure. Data is continually changing as it moves between your business, your clients, your employees, and your vendors. Your business data is in a continuous state of flux.

Create Your Business Data Strategy

Why do you have a data strategy? Just like other parts of your business, a strategy with a plan helps you to manage your business data. Your data strategy helps to prevent duplication across your business, allows for data unification, and defines your metrics or service level requirements. Your business data is a business asset you need to manage and protect. You need to identify multiple sources of data. Today your business data is a strategic advantage. You use your business data to improve your business processes, create new smart products and/or services, and **WOW** your clients, your employees, and your vendors.

The amount of data in our businesses is growing at a rapid pace. New opportunities to increase insights into your business by combining data are accelerating. This gives you the capability to see innovative ways to improve your business operations, your business strategy and to **WOW** your clients, your employees, and your vendors experience with your business. Therefore, it's more important than ever in the history of business to have a data strategy on how you access, manage, and leverage the data you create in your day-to-day business.

With a good business data strategy, you focus on knowing your clients so you service them appropriately. Today your clients expect a seamless user experience at all times. Knowing your business data gives you the ability to service clients on all the channels they may want to use. Having multiple channels for your client interactions is more complicated and requires you to understand your clients buying behaviours on all those channels.

It's key to your business data strategy to develop and implement a plan for data governance and to include change management. You need to maintain an audit trail of the information you use in your business decisions. Today's requirements for security and compliance means you need to identify, separate, and protect your business data, whether it's for privacy or financial reporting. Features such as confidentiality, integrity, and obtainability matter. Data classification is a must for any successful data security and compliance strategy. Your business data is an asset used in many of your business processes and your business applications. You need to organize your business data coherently to effectively manage your data across your business systems and business processes.

These are some of the questions I ask my clients when figuring out what their business data strategy is:

- What data do you require to run your business?
- How do you make your vision, your values, your goals, and your priorities align with your data?
- How often does your data need to be refreshed or updated?
- How are you going to store your data?
- What is your data archiving criteria – when to archive and for how long?
- How are you going to access your data – does it need to be real-time or is it not time-critical?
- How are you going to share your business data across your business?
- What are your Key Performance Indicators?
- Where and when do you need your business data?
- Do you have business data you use in various channels?
- Do you have a value for your business data?

Remember, our world is rapidly changing. Today's innovative businesses are using their data to understand client preferences and behaviours. These businesses are your competitors. They will outperform your business when they're using their business data more effectively than you're using yours.

Your business data is one of the most valuable assets of your business as it drives your business decisions. Good decisions lead to business growth. Your business will grow faster with a good business data strategy.

Model Your Business Data

What is a **Business Data Model (BDM)**? It's a representation of the business elements important to your business. A BDM is represented visually. A BDM organizes your business data elements and shows how they relate to each other. It provides a powerful method to communicate your business needs.

Let's say you're selling a car – some of the data elements you might want to know are the price, model, colour, year built, etc. Or when bringing on a new client – you may want to know the address, phone number, email address, etc.

A BDM supports your business processes, policies, procedures, and rules. Modelling your business data helps you to understand and communicate clearly about your business. It defines your business ideas, your business objects and their associations. It's wise to create your business data model early on in the development of your business model. It will help you greatly in understanding your business and communicating this understanding to your clients, your employees, and your vendors. Data models are the axis around which processes are specified to create, read, update, and delete your business data. All your business solutions (automated or not) will have requirements for business data.

Your BDM is a living document. As your business grows and changes, keep your BDM up-to-date. It's best to keep your BDM where it's accessed easily by those who manage it. You use the same data across all your business systems (whether automated or not) to share data seamlessly. Small changes in your business rules (the way you conduct your business) can be large changes in your business systems. You classify your business data in a clear and easy to understand way to diminish misunderstanding and duplication.

In a typical business, you have at the most 4 data models, a conceptual, a logical, a physical, and an enterprise. They each serve different purposes.

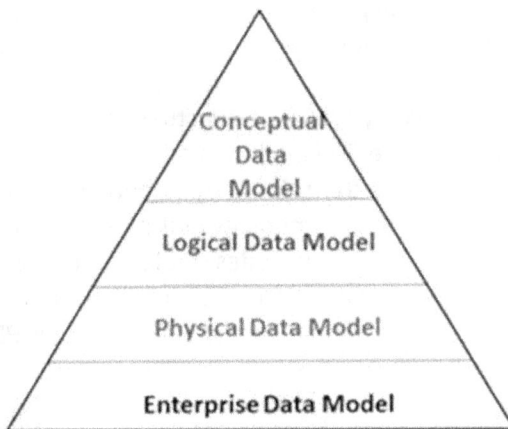

Figure 10 - Four Business Data Models

The **Conceptual Data Model (CDM)** represents your business ideas, business objects, and their associations. It's purely a business view. You use a CDM to look at your whole business, but typically it's used to look at specific areas of your business. You may have a CDM for client service, for operations, for finance or Accounts Payable or Accounts Receivable, etc. A CDM models your business objects like your clients, your employees, your vendors, your physical business location if you have one, your business assets, etc., and the attributes you associate with those objects. The data may be shared across your CDMs, like your client data, which may be found in several places in your business. This is the simplest of all the models, with business names so everyone across your business clearly understands. CDMs are good for presenting business cases to make changes in your business and also to help you with business planning.

The **Logical Data Model (LDM)** is a more in-depth look at your business data. You may have several LDMS aligned to your CDMS. Some of the data elements may be shared across your LDMS just as they are in your CDMS. LDMs are just an expanded view of your CDMs. Your entities (business objects) show their relationships to each other. Your business objects and attributes have definitions and you may include metadata. Metadata describes other data. Metadata describes how, when, and by whom data is gathered and formatted. The design of the tables (business objects), columns (business attributes), and keys (business relationships) is structural metadata. Descriptive metadata is for identification and discovery. Your LDMs are the connection of what your business wants and how your intended solution will implement it.

The **Physical Data Model (PDM)** is the actual physical blueprint design of your business database. This is how your database is designed and created. Your PDM shows the relationships between your data tables. Your PDM is dependent on technology – it's used in your automated business systems. Your PDM includes tables, columns, primary and foreign keys, data types, validation rules, triggers, stored procedures, etc. Your PDM uses more defined specific names. Your PDM is defined by the database software you use.

The **Enterprise Data Model (EDM)** is the unified view of all your business data produced and used across your entire business and the rules governing this data. Your EDM:

- Is independent of the technologies you have or don't have.
- Provides a common, consistent view and understanding of your data, the data elements, and their relationships throughout your whole business.
- Doesn't relate to how your data is sourced, accessed, stored or processed.
- Represents strategic information like your accounts, your products, your services, your clients, your policies, etc.
- Is useful for estimating, planning, and prioritizing your business initiatives.

"The new source of power is not money in the hands of a few, but information in the hands of many."
John Naisbitt

I have a story about business data and a very large bank in Canada. This bank decided to do an enterprise-wide project, their very first one. This bank had at least four different business units – Personal Banking, Commercial Banking, Personal Wealth Management, and Commercial Wealth Management with varying divisions underneath. I was tasked with synthesizing the data from 22 different automated systems so the data was fed into one new system, processed and then returned to the 22 systems it came from.

As I synthesized the data, I noticed a pattern, which wasn't favourable. As I looked at the business data collected from these 22 different systems, I saw not all the systems collected the same data for the bank's clients. The data provided different views of the client, but nowhere was there one standard view which allowed for a total understanding of the client or what I call a 360 view.

This isn't a good place to be in your business as you cannot really serve your clients well, when they have to go to different places in your business to manage their business with you. You're leaving potential revenue on the table or in the client's hands.

The preferable technique to set-up your client data is one record of data to one client, ensuring this data is centralized and available to all users and systems (automated or not) that your business uses. With this solution, you provide a better client experience, one which will **WOW** your clients. The one data record – one client is easier for your employees to manage both up-sales and cross-sales to your clients.

As you understand and apply each data model to your business, you will find the more you use your business data to make money, the more business data you acquire, which in turn helps you to make more money in the future. Structure your business data so you extract the pertinent sought-after insights to help you monetize. Guess what, I'm going to next take you on a journey to explore various ways to monetize from your business data.

Monetize Your Business Data

You want to have your business data work for you. Have you given any thought to improving your business margins? Did you know your business data helps you to cut costs while increasing your revenues? Let's look at how your business data is monetized. This happens when your actual business data is your product or service, or your business data helps to drive your business revenues or your business data helps to improve your profit margins.

How do you do this? Other businesses will pay to have your business data, so you sell it to them or you make it accessible through your business and you sell it via a membership or a subscription program. As you get to **Know Your Client (KYC)** you improve your products and/or services to increase your client's **WOW** experience. When you have a large source of content, you use it to drive ads or find ways to drive your clients through your sales funnel or to have targeted advertising. You use your business data to optimize your sales funnel conversion or your prices or have a more accurate prediction of your supply and demand.

What are some steps to help you uncover these ways to monetize your business data? I always encourage my clients to start with the 6 W questions – **Who, What, Where, When, Why,** and **How**. Look for patterns in your business data. Is there something someone is doing with your business data where you can make a targeted offer, or you see a lack of variation in your business data when you analyse it that you draw relevant conclusions, or you connect data from different sources to create a new more valuable view, or you add new external data to your existing business data? You require good analytic skills, if you don't have them in-house, outsource them.

> *"The most valuable commodity I know of is information."*
> Gordon Gekko, Wall Street

Here are a few ideas on ways to monetize your business data. You can:

- Sell or trade your client data.
- Use your client data to create new products and/or services.
- Use your client data to make smart, targeted marketing decisions on 'who to offer what'.
- Segment your clients to present better offers, plus up-sell and cross-sell when you have data like demographics, client interests, and buying and browsing behaviours.
- Use your web visitor data to convert prospects who already have an interest in your business. A prospect who just met you requires multiple touches before they make a buy decision.
- Analyse client data to tell you where your clients are, what they want, and how you present it.
- Use your client data to provide more specific ads targeting your prospective clients.
- Use your transaction data to optimize your pricing.
- Build content and use your client engagement data to determine what content to provide.
- Create a larger engagement using behavioural data with improved content recommendations and charge for using.
- Use conversion and purchase data to influence your pricing.
- Sell memberships or subscriptions to premium data.
- Sell development access to your raw business data.
- Build industry specific predictive models.
- Build an app to collect data and help clients at the same time.
- Have more useful and more accurate insights into how to improve your business.
- Use your operational data to help you streamline your operations process getting your products out the door to your clients' faster.

Looking at the different ways you monetize your business data, you see there are many different types of data in your business. Let's look at those next.

Business Data Types & Sources

There are several types of data and their sources that are important for you to know.

Identity data is a unique identifier which enables all other data types to be connected, making descriptions, comparisons, contrasts and relationships to be known. The heart of your sales and marketing efforts is based on knowing who your individual client is. You want to capture data like name, birth date, gender, address, telephone, email, social media, account information, etc.

Descriptive data is all the objective data used to describe the identity. This is demographic information such as family facts like marital status, # of children, and ages of children, etc., lifestyle facts like dwelling type, car type, pets, etc., career facts like profession or business, education completed, etc.

Quantitative data helps you to understand how your client behaves, what transactions they made with your business and how they've reacted to your business. This data is about any activity between your client and your business. It can be online or offline transaction data on the number and type of product purchases, the monetary value, order and renewal dates, abandoned sales, returns, etc. You want the data from your clients' online activities such as visits to your website, the products and/or services they view, what they download, etc. You want data from your business social media activities such as Facebook business page likes, Twitter communications, comments on articles you post on places like LinkedIn or blog posts. You want the data from your clients' service interactions such as complaints, feedback, praise, inquiries, etc.

Qualitative data is usually gathered from surveys or questionnaires where you gauge attitudes, motivation or opinion. Attitude questions can be how they rate your client service or your products, or how likely they are to buy from you again. Motivation questions can be what was the reason for purchasing the product – for yourself or a gift, or a key reason for the product purchase – like the type of product, or the quality or the price. Opinion questions can be about your clients' likes and dislikes.

When you classify your business data and relate it to your vision, your values, your goals, and your prioritiesfor your business, you quickly identify the business data which provides the critical information for your business success. When you aren't sure if you need to keep a piece of data, it's better to be safe than sorry. You can delete it later if it turns out it wasn't used by your business.

> *"You can have data without information,*
> *but you cannot have information without data."*
> Daniel Keys Moran

What are some of the ways you collect this business data? There are two sources for the business data you want, internal and external. You collect internal business data from sales, marketing, human resources, and finance. Internal business data helps you to know what business strategies are working or do you get innovative and make some changes. You collect internal business data through forms, surveys, questionnaires, and interviews. Some companies collect business data through user comments. You collect your business data by looking at your clients' behaviours when they interact with your business. Sales data comes from revenue and profit from distribution channels, price points, geographic locations, types of clients, and of course, the salesperson. Finance provides business data on costs, your vendors, and your cash flow: what money is coming in and what money is going out. Marketing data can be website statistics, promotions, advertising, etc. Human resources will give you data on your employees.

There are two sources of external data, primary and secondary. Primary business data is data collected from original sources such as salesmen and clients. It can be a slow process, but this business data is usually more correct and dependable. Secondary business data are obtained from newspapers, journals, business magazines, government publications and reports, trade associations, published surveys and reports from independent research firms, foreign governments, international agencies, colleges, universities and libraries.

Making Decisions With Data

Data-Driven Decision Making (DDDM) is about assembling business data to assist you to better understand your business and use that understanding to make improvements in your business. This kind of decision making has you looking at the patterns in your business, asking questions about these patterns and investigating them. This way you're making decisions based on evidence and verifiable business data.

DDDM is a method used to gain a competitive lead. Assimilating enormous quantities of business data from different business areas and deriving actionable business data can be easier said than done. One of the best ways to start this process is to conduct an analysis of your current business state. Next, you want to look at questions to ask to provide opportunities for business improvement that you can measure and test. You make decisions on just about anything with the right amount of business data from developing products to hiring to advertising to income projections, etc.

After you have asked your questions, you create a plan with theories, you collect your business data, you analyse to gain insights and based on your analysis, you make recommendations. You may have heard of A/B or split testing for optimizing websites. However, did you know with enough business data, any repeatable, measurable business process can be conducted as an A/B test? The best way to find the optimal business processes in your business is to have continuous testing.

> *"The goal is to turn data into information,*
> *and information into insight."*
> Carly Fiorina

You start by optimizing your business processes. Pick a regular business activity that can be measured. List all the characteristics for doing the activity well. Every time this activity is performed, note the value of each characteristic and how it turned out. When you have a sensible number of data points, go back and compare the different characteristics with their outcomes. Some characteristics forecast success, others forecast failure, and the rest won't have any predictive value. You include your new knowledge into the business activity.

Here are some examples of areas where you use DDDM. When you collect client data for each client, you're able to find out which leads you want to go after. You use criteria such as what do your largest accounts have in common or what clients had the quickest sales and then look for similar leads. By being aware of the patterns of behaviour you create targeted sales. You use this for better hiring by knowing where your employee came from, who their interviewer was, and what their performance has been like over a period of time. You're able to know things like how must each marketing channel costs per lead and how quickly they purchase. When you're looking for investment money, you track where you meet potential investors and what type of investors they are.

The more you're monitoring independent characteristics, the greater your understanding is. Be careful not to over simplify because your sample collection is too small. Starting collecting your business data early. It's better to have raw business data than already processed business data. To improve your understanding, connect your business data with as many independent data sources as you find.

While building up a huge dataset is great, there are things that reduce the value of your business data. Can you find other, simpler ways to gather your business data? You want to keep your costs down. Is your business data clean and accurate? Messy business data isn't an accurate picture. Is your business data fresh or stale? Stale business data has less usefulness.

I've given you an overview about your business data; why it's important to understand your business data and how it helps you be innovative in today's competitive marketplace. Next I want to look at the **People** around your business; your clients, your employees, and your vendors.

CHAPTER 7
THEY'RE DRIVING YOU MAD

ശ൫ൻ൫ൽ൫ശ൫ൻ൫ൽ

How Do They Find You?

Your business is started with a fantastic product and/or service, but it doesn't operate in a vacuum. You need people who are going to be your clients, your employees, and your vendors. What are you going to do to find them?

The first thing you do is get clear on your vision, your values, your goals, and your priorities. You get the word out into the marketplace about you and your business. You want everyone to know what you're doing.

You're good at what you do, so become a respected expert resource, the go-to person in your industry. You write a book to brand you, just like I did with this one. Start or join a Meet up group. Write articles and post them on LinkedIn. Or start a blog with authentic help and while you're at it, talk about the businesses you respect and say why – you never know they might reciprocate. Make a memorable video and post it all over social media. Stand out – don't be like everyone else. Focus on what makes you different. Link to charity, make sure you give back to your community. Start discussions with your targets and make sure you're listening.

Make sure you have a media kit with a great press release. I can help you create this, so you reach out to media, journalists, reporters, researchers, trade magazines, reviewers, bloggers, retailers, websites, internet, radio and/or television shows, editors, event coordinators, potential clients, potential partners or anyone who is interested in you.

Do you live in the city? There's a lot of activity in the city. Find networking groups, reach out to co-working places, get involved in local events. Get creative, think outside the box. If you drive – brand your car with your business logo – every time you go somewhere you have free advertising.

Go to events or conferences where you have the opportunity to meet lots of people and share your business with them. See if you can speak at these events. Check with your Chamber of Commerce or your City Hall. Work with recruiters, universities, colleges, and high schools to find employees. Ask everyone you know or who you meet for referrals when looking for your clients, employees or vendors.

When you meet someone at an event, a conference, a Meetup, or some other venue and they want to connect with you, take their business card, but for goodness sakes, do the follow-up. Reach out to them, find out what challenges they're having in their business or their personal life.

When your business doesn't solve their problem, refer them to someone who does solve their problem. You're then remembered for being helpful. Do joint ventures with other businesses who have a similar audience. Hold events together.

> *"Surround yourself with good people who encourage and love you. There are always ups and downs, no matter how successful you are."*
> Liana Liberato

Get involved in social media. Learn which social media is best for your business type. See where your competition hangs out. Post relevant information on a regular frequency. Connect and respond when people reach out to these channels.

Establish your presence online with a great website. Make sure you have A/B split testing done. Find out about Search Engine Optimization (SEO) – make sure Google finds you and finds you near the top of the search, if not first. Make sure your website is optimized for mobile viewing on a tablet or smart phone.

There are a lot of different ways in our world today to reach out, connect, and be seen. Be genuine, be authentic, be yourself, get the word out about who you are, and what you want.

Celebrate Your Clients

Ok, you now have clients. You want your clients to have the best experience when they interact with you and your business. You want them to have a **WOW** experience so over the top, they keep coming back. How do you do this? Let me give you a few tips on ways to impact and **WOW** your clients:

Be Careful with Your Language– Make sure you hold your clients in high esteem. Speak in a respectful manner to them and about them. All your words are a reflection of you and your business. Know your client's name and use it often.

Communicate, Communicate, Communicate - Your clients want to hear from you. They want to know they are number one and very important to you. Build a strong relationship with your clients so they're always delighted to hear from you. Don't just call them to sell to them, call them to see how they are, how their business is, and ask if they have any challenges you can help them with. Be upfront and honest, but do it with respect. Ask the difficult questions, always be willing to help, and always do what you know is right even if you lose the client. Your integrity is more important. Never tell your clients not to worry, take the time to educate them.

Communicate In-Person – Know when to communicate in-person with your clients. If it's important, pick up the phone, or better still, make an in-person meeting. Don't do the important stuff by email or text.

Set Big Goals – Set your sights on the target and then aim even higher to deliver products and/or services your clients will never forget. When you aim high enough and give your clients a **WOW** experience, they will tell others.

Be Proactive – Be the first to make the phone call. Constantly update your clients, keeping them informed all the way through the sale or the project. Always direct your clients to what needs to be done next. You stay in the driver's seat and in control of your clients' experience with you and your business.

Do the Personal Touch – Remember the social niceties – give a hand-written note or card for an occasion important to your client. Everyone loves to be remembered.

Show Respect – Treat all your clients with respect, even when you have to say no. Say no and provide the explanation. Really listen to your clients and ask questions to make sure you really understand their wants and needs. Always be professional. And if a client disrespects you, then you know what to do – end the relationship as soon as it's feasible.

Be Open about Potential Issues – Always tell your clients about issues with advance notice or as soon as you know. Involve them in finding solutions. Give them the advantage of your knowledge.

Hold Your Clients in High Regard – Your clients are paying you to help them solve challenges or issues in their business or personal life. Make sure you give them everything you have. Don't hold back.

Ask for Feedback – Ask your clients if they are happy with your products and/or services. If they aren't happy, don't let it go; get to the bottom of it, find out what went wrong and then go about fixing it.

"There is only one boss. The client.
And he can fire everybody
in the company from the chairman on down,
simply by spending his money somewhere else. "
Sam Walton

You create client loyalty when you treat your clients with respect, are positive, and go above and beyond to address any issue quickly and efficiently. A satisfied happy client spreads positive words about your business. Remember, you compete by giving your clients the white glove personal attention and care - the **WOW**.

Client Relationship Management

You might have a few clients or many; however, it doesn't matter how many, you still have to manage them. The Canadian banks have a principle called **Know Your Client (KYC)**. It's absolutely imperative you know your client thoroughly. This means really listening to your client and keeping great notes on what your client tells you.

How do you do this? When you're starting out, use an Excel spreadsheet, or a Microsoft Access database, or use **Client Relationship Management (CRM)** software. I'm not going to give CRM recommendations only because technology is constantly changing and what was great today may not be great tomorrow or whenever you read this.

CRM is much more than capturing information about your current and prospective clients. CRM is a methodology to know your clients by assembling data from a variety of contacts with your business. This client data can be from their website, phone calls, emails, chats, marketing, social media, or meetings and may include notes and action items, documents, presentations, personal information, buying history and preferences, client service calls, conversion and growth strategies, client satisfaction, etc.

You analyse your client data to look for patterns to help you to find your high tier clients, ways to improve your client relationships, ways to cross-sell or up-sell, ways to drive retention, and increase your business sales.

CRM has many benefits. You understand your clients, provide **WOW** experiences, attract and win new clients, lower your costs, improve your client communications, manage targeted marketing, decrease response times, and serve a wider area. Another wonderful benefit is you won't have to be looking in a variety of places such as your files or emails or texts for all your valuable client data as you will have it all in one easily accessible place. Anyone in your business can have a complete history of all your client interactions. Now your client conversations are current, personal, and pertinent, which is a **WOW** client experience.

Clients today want a personalized, efficient buying experience from start to finish. They're busy, when they call into your business, they don't have time to be kept on hold or transferred around. You're able to target your marketing and sales efforts to the right clients, the ones who want your products and/or services. You're busy building and growing your business. You quickly identify what you're doing right and use this knowledge to improve and grow. The best thing for your business is for you to be performing the activities only you're capable of to make your cash register ring and not spend your time on administrative details like capturing, analysing, and preparing reports.

When you invest in CRM, you have the people who interact with your clients entering the client data. The CRM system analyses and creates reports based on the analysis. You see your sales pipeline. Is it working, are there any difficulties, etc.? You know information about your sales teams and who is the most industrious. You find out if there are a lot of complaints about specific products and/or services. Do these complaints fall into specific categories which allows you to address issues more promptly?

You learn about your client services, how responsive they are, how quickly they solve the client's issues, what are the top client issues, etc. Your business is on the same page about your clients as you have a common platform to provide your client view, and the more information you have, the more you have a 360 view of your clients.

You believe you don't need a CRM; and that you manage your business quite well with email, a calendar, and a to-do list. Let me assure you, you're not seeing the whole picture. With all of your client data in one system, you have a 360 view. You're more informed about your clients and your business. An organized business is a successful business.

Client WOWs

Over the years I've worked with a variety of industries and clients. I was influenced by a poster I saw when I was a young waitress. It's a picture of a lion with a crown on his head and the caption above his head reads: **Your Customer is King** and below him reads: **Without a Customer, YOU have No Paycheque.** This was the start of my journey to learn how to interact with my clients. I've had many great client experiences and some not so great client experiences. However, I've always been able to turn my client's experience with me into a **WOW**.

People love to be treated with dignity and respect. There are many ways to do this. My gran always told me everyone, no matter who they were or what they did in life, deserved to be treated kindly. It didn't matter whether they were the Queen or a homeless person on the street.

This story isn't a client story per se, but it's an example of how by taking a little time to listen, you uncover a wealth of knowledge. At 21, I left my island home in Victoria, British Columbia to go to school on the mainland in Vancouver. The school provided housing in an apartment building where the first three floors were a seniors' residence.

I came in or out of the lobby between the hours of 5:00 pm to 7:00 pm almost every day. An older gentleman was always sitting in the lobby. After a few weeks, we started to make eye contact, then smiles, and finally hellos. After a few more weeks, I started to stop and sit a few moments with my new-found friend. At the time, this lovely 97-year-old was the oldest person I knew.

After a few days, he started to open up, telling me stories of his life. He'd had and lost a couple of large fortunes in his day, but this never stopped him from experiencing life. He taught me success isn't how much money you have, how many houses or cars or other material things, but how much you interact with life, making memories. I want you to remember when you're working with your clients that you're making memories for both your client and yourself, so make them memorable; make them a **WOW**.

I worked at EDS for a short time on the help desk for an Electronic Data Interchange (EDI) solution. One day I received a phone call from the florist who served EDS at their headquarters in Plano, Texas. He had a small, nagging problem which never seemed to get resolved on his calls to the helpdesk. I didn't stop until I found the solution, which didn't take very long when I became laser focused on his problem. He was very happy at the end of the call. I was pleased to have solved his long-standing issue. The next day when I came into work, I didn't see my desk. Why? Because it was covered with the largest bouquet of flowers to say thank-you. No one had ever received flowers before. I gave this client a **WOW** experience.

I learned the power of knowing people's names, taking the time to talk to them, really listening, and learning about them while at EDS. I used to get to know everyone, the garbage person, the receptionist, the person who delivered the mail, etc. It didn't matter what you did; if you came into my world, I wanted to know who you were and how you were. My colleagues used to tease me about why was I spending time with those they thought were beneath me. I didn't think this and just continued. Lo and behold, there were many times I needed a last-minute rush on a package or an impromptu lunch ordered or a big mess cleaned up. Guess what? I always received the help I required. A greeting, a name, and a smile go a long way to make someone's day.

Laurie K. Grant

Another client from the EDS helpdesk was a woman who worked for a tie manufacturer. She was always angry and never felt her problems were solved to her satisfaction. I discovered the best way was to really listen, to paraphrase back what she wanted, and to get her off the phone to allow her time to become **CALM** by finding one little thing to quickly investigate.

I called her back in 20–30 minutes with an answer and explained the other issues take more time to resolve. I gave her an email update every day until the problem was resolved. She was so happy to finally be heard and communicated with, she only spoke to me. She didn't let anyone else handle her call when I was away from the office, preferring to wait until I returned. She was only angry with me on the very first call.

These are just a few small examples to give you some ideas on how you create **WOW** experiences for your clients. I hope they inspire you.

Steer Your Vendors

Your vendors are another important set of people in your business. They make or break you, as you're dependent on them to provide products and/or services. You want to have **WOW** vendor relationships. Locating a dependable and competitively-priced vendor is necessary for your business success. You want to find vendors who have quality products and/or services that meet or exceed your business requirements. Building mutually beneficial relationships with your vendors goes a long way to helping your business.

It pays to inform yourself about any vendor you're thinking of using. You require an understanding of their business to assess the value they're providing you. Meet with your vendors at the beginning of your relationship and at regular intervals as long as you're using them for your business. Make sure you pass any referrals along. When negotiating, see if you get a better deal by offering exclusivity. However, make sure you perform timely reviews of your vendors and know what other opportunities exist elsewhere.

Do you need a contract or a **Service Level Agreement (SLA)**? Some vendors won't do business with you without one. SLAs are important when you have a dependency on the vendor to meet your client's needs. Be careful of signing contracts for a specified time-period with no get-out clause. This locks you in and when the vendor's service is poor, you're stuck paying them until the end of the contract term. You want a clearly defined set of expectations that includes rewards and penalties.

Some things to negotiate when creating your contract or SLA are how and when you pay; what, if any, are additional costs; and are there potential risks – what happens when you're late making a payment or, conversely, what happens when they deliver faulty, late or not all products and/or services. I learned the hard way not all vendors are truthful, authentic people who want to serve you well. Some are just in it for the money.

Regular communication with scheduled meetings and having goals identified goes a long way to make your vendor relationships work well. In your vendormeetings, it's a good idea to focus on critical concerns and ways you or the vendor can improve the relationship. Focus on what you and the vendor can do to lower costs, which means you give them more business.

Plan well in advance, so you're giving your vendors sufficient lead time. Don't continually change your order once it's delivered to the vendor. Just like you don't want painful clients, you don't want to be a painful client. Share important information as soon as you know it. Be honest, be upfront, don't hide things; it just makes matters worse when the truth finally comes out.

> *"The reason I grew so fast in the supermarket business, without*
> *help of the banks in those days, was through my vendors.*
> *I convinced my vendors, the companies I was doing business with,*
> *if I did more business, they would do more business."*
> John Catsimatidis

Planning makes for good vendor relationships. Plan ahead for emergencies. Remember Murphy's Law – *"Anything that can go wrong, will go wrong."* It's helpful to have an agreement in place on how you and your vendors handle emergencies. When you do experience an emergency, analyse it afterwards to see how to avoid it in the future.

With a little foresight, you can manage disastrous situations smoothly.

You like to get paid on time, well, guess what; so, do your vendors. Giving them the excuse the cheque is in the mail when it isn't, is just downright dishonest. When you continually pay late, you run the risk that your vendor won't give you a great deal in the future or you end up lower on their priority list when you want something in a hurry. Have a system to forecast your supply requirements. Use your system to budget your sales and your payments. This way you never have unhappy vendors.

There are many reasons for contract terminations by either yourself or your vendor. You fire the vendor for constantly failing to provide you with your required products and/or service, or you found a less expensive or a more dependable vendor. Conversely, your vendor fires you for too many late payments or continually making changes to orders. It's important to treat your vendors as well as you do your clients and your employees.

Vendor Relationship Management

You have clients, and you have vendors who help you to serve products and/or services to those clients. Today's global economy is very competitive with many things to contemplate when selecting a vendor. And it doesn't stop just because you selected them; you have to manage the relationship. You want to get the best value from the investment of your time and money. The best way to do this is with **Vendor Relationship Management (VRM)**.

VRM is a methodology and tools for strategically managing your vendor interactions. You make quick, well-informed decisions with impressive results. This allows you to maximize the value of your vendor relationships and to minimize the business risk during the lifetime of your connection to any particular vendor. It allows you to capture value after the ink has dried on your vendor contracts.

Today, in business, the focus is on the relationships you build. Good relationships with your vendors can make your business, just as bad relationships can kill your business. Which one do you want? Good; glad to hear you chose the good relationship. Let's look at some ways to make it happen. You earn trust with your vendors by having honest and open communication, understanding their world, and involving them in your business, thereby, making them an entrusted partner in your business.

Your vendor relationships work best when they're equally advantageous to both parties. Being in alignment provides greater achievements, less risks, improved co-operation, and improvements in business innovation. With a successful VRM implementation you expect to have the benefits of a quicker time to get your products and/or services to your clients, increased transactional effectiveness, being more competitive, managed risk, and improved finances, which all contributes to your overall profit. This means you deliver quality products and/or services ahead of the market.

You must remember, both you and your vendor have businesses to manage. Just as you're assessing your vendor's performance, they're also assessing you. You may want to take a look at how many vendors you have. Too many is overwhelming, difficult to manage, leads to inefficiencies, and higher administrative cost. With less vendors, you have closer relationships where you work together to control expenses. When your vendors are giving you grief, it's time to let them go. You and your employees don't need the headache. One of the ways I tell my clients to figure out which vendors to let go is to conduct a performance evaluation. Look at their reliability, on time deliveries, costs, communication, etc.

VRM works hand in hand with strategic sourcing. It's a detailed analysis to align your business to managing vendors based on clearly defined and documented relationship strategies. Another fantastic VRM strategy is to invite your vendors to your business. Include them in your procurement meetings. Invite them to your business events and parties. Provide them with timely information whenever you have a new product and/or service or a new employee. You also want to visit your vendors' businesses and learn about how their businesses run. This creates a more solid business relationship.

As your business grows, it's a wise decision to invest in VRM software. Your best bet is a system which makes it easy to view and analyse your vendors. It's convenient to have vendor profiles and to monitor their performance.

You want to run your business efficiently and having an operational VRM methodology and software in place goes a long way to help achieve this. Effective VRM not only provides huge savings, but it also brings you giant opportunities.

Employee Relationship Management

Ok, I've shown you CRM and VRM. Did you know there's also **Employee Relationship Management (ERM)**? ERM is a methodology you use to manage all your employee interactions effectively. Your employees are the chief assets of your business. You want them to work as a team and contribute to the realization of your vision, your values, your goals, and your priorities. ERM activities help to make a cohesive bond for all the employees who work in your business.

ERM provides for a variety of activities connecting the relationship between your business and your employees. ERM has inputs from both you and your employees to align your day-to-day business. Some reasons for putting an ERM in place are because you want to:

- Reduce your employee turnover.
- Treat your employees fairly and justly.
- Measure productivity, which aids in knowing when and where to hire.
- Manage employee training, development, and discipline.
- Conduct employee evaluations and have employees evaluate their workplace.
- Manage the benefits you provide ensuring they are valued by your employees.
- Encourage great employee morale and loyalty to your business.
- Foster an environment for creative and innovative thinking.
- Provide a business culture where your employees thrive.
- Abide by all the applicable employment laws for the locations your business operates in.
- Define the benchmarks and qualifications for each job role.
- Provide a work-life balance.

Some of the areas where you use ERM are:

New Hire On-boarding – Where you introduce new employees to your business so they learn the actions, information, and abilities to function effectively in your business.

Training – Where you provide mentorship, specific on-the-job activities (job shadowing, growth projects), and professional development (conferences, events, schooling, leadership training courses, etc.)

Compensation – Where you manage payroll, cheques, bank account deposits, statements, starting salary, increases, bonuses, incentives, benefits, awards, education expense, loans or pay advances, business expense reimbursement, sick leave, holiday time off, overtime, profit sharing, shares, etc.

Recruitment – Where you create job roles and skill sets required, job postings, source and screen candidates, conduct resume analysis, conduct candidate testing, interview, analyse interview results, prepare job offers, conduct background and reference checks, present job offers, etc.

Career management – Where you create career progression roadmaps, create job roles with core responsibilities, and skills required, classify fundamental proficiencies and predicted performance, establish rules for performance accountability, evaluations of employees and by employees of your business, etc.

Time management – Where you share your vision, your values, your goals, and your priorities to your employees to follow, ensure there is both short and long term objectives to meet, ensure productivity quotas, monitor employee performance, comply with labour laws regarding time worked, overtime, vacation, sick time, daily breaks, shifts including trades and cancellations, flex time, job sharing, arrival and departure times, etc.

Above all else, keep open and transparent communication with all your employee policies and practices. Next I want to explore the many ways to find the **Knowledge** you require to run a successful business.

CHAPTER 8

LACK OF KNOWLEDGE

ణ్ణ

What Knowledge Do You Need?

You have a great business idea, you know you can do this, but there are some things to know and do before you hang out your shingle (sign). When you start your business without the knowledge you require to be a success, there's a strong chance your business won't make it. Let's explore what you need to know. It pays to do your homework, take stock of what you do and don't know, and make a plan to either acquire or hire for what you don't know.

The most important piece is doing the market research first. Why? Because then you know there's a market demand for your products and/or services. How are you going to finance your venture? The startup costs are staggering. And even if you buy a franchise, you still need to find the (quite often) hefty down payment. You select a business model to use to take your products and/or services to the marketplace. Is it scalable? Is it flexible? Does it handle rapid growth when you're a success? You also plan an exit strategy.

Ok, even after all of the above, you still want to follow your dream and make it a reality. Here are some questions to ponder on. Are you a glass half-full or half-empty person, or better still, a glass refillable? Being optimistic is a trait that gets you through the difficult times. It won't be all roses, there are some thorns along the way. Are you a big picture person? Do you have a vision you clearly articulate in a compelling way to inspire others to participate with your vision?

Do you take initiative to solve your issues? Do you like to lead, to make decisions, and to take action? Are you driven to realize your dreams? Do you tolerate taking risks along the way? Are you able to bounce back quickly after something goes awry? Do you look at your errors and disasters to learn from them? What kind of interpersonal skills do you have? Do you lead? Do you delegate? Are you able to listen? Do you communicate effectively in a variety of formats? Do you negotiate or barter? Have you got the ethics to treat everyone involved with your business with dignity, respect, fairness, integrity, and truth?

How are your thinking skills? Do you see more than one solution to an issue? Do you think outside the box and come up with new innovative ways to serve your clients? Do you recognize opportunities as they present themselves? Do you make plans and stick to them? Do you set your vision, your values, your goals, and your priorities, and schedule for them? Do you make decisions and take action on those decisions?

It's helpful to have a broad knowledge of sales, marketing, finance, operations, client service, and when they're not your area of expertise, then hire those who have this expertise. Until you find the right business model for you, acquire knowledge in raising capital, or experiment. What do you know about your market space and how you're going to deliver your products and/or services? Have you worked in this field before? Do you have any prior expertise?

As you see, there's a lot to think about, understand, and know before you launch your business. All the drive and determination in the world won't benefit you when you don't have the required knowledge to lead a successful business. You must research and plan according to what you discover. However, there are very few people who have all the skills required when they first start out. There are many different hats to wear. I believe the most important thing to be successful is to have the want, the drive, and the ability to listen to others who have gone before you, to be willing to learn, and to be willing to change to move your business forward.

Let's explore a few different ways you might gain the knowledge needed to get your bright, shiny idea off the ground and out the door.

Going Back to School

Going back to school is one way to acquire the knowledge required to run your business and take your bright, shiny idea out into the world. Here are some options on how you obtain this education.

When you're young, just leaving high school or in your early 20's, consider college or university. There are many different business degrees available today. They provide a wide selection of learning choices with diverse outcomes. Some of these choices are purely academic theory, whereas others are practical hands-on learning, and still others are a mixture of academic and hands-on learning. These are further differentiated by undergraduate, graduate or professional.

These degrees give you a solid grounding in business operations and allow you to specialize in areas such as client service, marketing, strategy, policy, sales, communications, etc. These skills are used in many areas of your life. They're not a waste of time if you decide later you don't want to be an entrepreneur. Some of the skills you gain are:

Accounting	Analysis & Problem Solving	Business Management	Communication, Presentation & Writing
Conflict Management	Decision Making & Logic	Finances & Economics	Marketing
Negotiation Skills	Project Management	Quality Control	Resource Management
Operations & Client Service	Strategy & Planning	Supply Chain Management	Time (Self) Management

"You're off to great places, today is your day,
your mountain is waiting, so get on your way."
Dr. Seuss

When you're not sure about a traditional MB, try a mini MBA. It provides a more structured environment and an important understanding of management practices, standards, and strategic tools. This offers a succinct approach to strengthen your performance, confidence, and decision-making. You're able to master core business concepts in a shorter timeframe. You have the opportunity to network with other business people from a variety of industries. There are three distinct flavours, the in-person fast track which allows you to gain great skills in a short time period, the elite pre-MBA which is an expensive way to check out a school to evaluate if you're interested in their MBA program, and lastly, the online MOOC (Massive Open Online Course) which will get you a basic knowledge of business practices and language.

Another area is online education. Many business programs are designed for entrepreneurs and some of them are free. In today's global markets and changing economies with constant changes in technologies, it's a daunting task to keep up. Online learning provides the necessary skills to manage the newest trends quicker and more easily than your traditional bricks and mortar schools. Many online classes are from schools with degrees, so the instructors have access to the same resources as the bricks and mortar professors do. Numerous online classes are structured so you complete them at your own pace.

Entrepreneurs are usually inventive business experts who start their own endeavours. They create businesses such as corporations, non-profits, and sole proprietorships. They're accountable for many business activities. Many business degrees deliver priceless internship prospects, where you obtain real-world business knowledge, valued contacts, and hands-on practice. I've shown you a few ways to find schooling to help you gain the skills you need to run your business successfully.

Empower Your Employees

We've looked at how to **WOW** your clients and your vendors; last, but not least, you want to empower and **WOW** your employees. When your employees are excited about your business vision, they make it their own and work enthusiastically towards making it a realized vision. A crucial factor for your business success is employees who are motivated and committed. You want to encourage your employees to **WOW** your clients by empowering them with the freedom to use their unique talents to serve your clients and your business.

As the leader and champion of your business, it's your role to make sure everything is in sync. Clearly communicate not only your vision, your values, your goals, and your priorities, but also the roles you expect your employees to perform. You want your employees to have the confidence and knowledge to make appropriate decisions. Be a good role model by listening, being sincere, being disciplined, celebrating your employees' accomplishments, and demonstrating a winner's positive attitude. Foster a culture of open communication; invite and welcome employee feedback.

Give your employees access to the tools needed to manage their roles. Keep your employees accountable; let them know when they meet your expectations. When your employees don't meet your expectations, take the time to listen, understand, and provide guidance to move them in the direction you want them to go. Make the most of their strengths and work to minimize their weaknesses. Allow them to think outside the box. Don't micromanage or hover. Don't ask your employees to do something you aren't willing to do yourself. You want them to have a mindset of independence, capability, and responsibility.

"Start with good people, lay out the rules,
communicate with your employee, motivate them and reward them.
If you do all those things effectively, you can't miss.
Lee Iacocca

Find out where your employees want to go and help them get there. Provide training, more responsibility, new opportunities for growth and enrichment or promotions into roles where they stretch. Don't forget to appreciate and recognize efforts, as well as, reward their successes. Be friendly; get to know who your employees are, never be too busy to say hello and talk with them. Be respectful of their time and acknowledge they have a life outside your business. Remember, life happens to everyone, so be flexible, and adjust as necessary. Don't be rude. Give more compliments than you give criticism. When you must criticize, do it constructively so your employees know what to do to improve.
Keep your employees informed about what your business is doing and where it's going. Involve them in planning and decision-making. You might be very surprised at the value, ideas, insights, and knowledge they bring to the table. Invite their feedback and suggestions for improvements. Remember, your way may not be the only way to achieve the desired end result. When you implement their feedback or suggestions, make sure to give them recognition. Public recognition goes a long way in making your employees feel WOW.

When you have a warm and friendly workplace, you have warm and friendly employees who treat your clients well. Provide team-building opportunities both inside and outside your workplace. These are good for bonding. Provide company-wide celebrations for successes and important holidays. Support time off. The last thing you want is a burnt-out workforce.

Remember, your employees are already empowered; what you're doing is giving them their voice. However, be advised you will have Chaos when your employees don't have the technical competency and organizational clarity to carry out their duties. Uphold your part of the employment equation and your employees will uphold their part.

Coaches & Mentors

Why do you want a business coach? Many times, your business issues aren't apparent to you. A coach helps you to see what's in your blind spot. They help you discover where you're lying to yourself and help you face the reality required to have a successful business. A coach is trained to look for your areas of potential and help you take advantage of them. Excellent performers in any field usually have a coach. A coach gives you the advantage of their experience. They ask you many more questions than they answer. They encourage you to contemplate your business in ways you might not be able to do on your own.

A good coach asks you questions you don't think to ask yourself, like:

- What do you really want?
- Why do you work so much?
- What has the most importance for you?
- What impacts do you want to have?

A good business coach helps you to:

- Understand where persistent complications come from
- Address your real business issues methodically and efficiently
- Manage your business more competently
- Decrease surplus, increase production, and grow a profitable business

The reason to use a coach is to become better at what you do. Don't go crazy looking for a coach from your industry. The best coach for you might know nothing about your business industry. Their perspective is very valuable because they're an outsider to your business. Things to look for in a business coach are: Experience, Attitude, Expertise, Accessibility, Feedback Ability, Passion, Delivery Style, Accountability.

"Our chief want is someone who will inspire us to
be what we know we could be."
Ralph Waldo Emerson

A business mentor is a professional with more business experience, who supports you to develop specific skills and knowledge outside your business expertise. Business mentors leverage their knowledge, wisdom, and experience by sharing and transferring to you their knowledge, experience, and skills. A business mentor is a guide and trusted confidant who assists you with finding the correct direction for your business and developing appropriate solutions. Mentoring is like coaching, but it's a larger, more holistic progression. Coaches have specialised training and credentials and are usually paid for their services, whereas mentors may not be. Mentors do it as a way to give back. Mentors have the opportunity to learn from you.

It's lonely at the top. A good sounding board or second opinion is valuable to learn from others' mistakes and successes. Mentors are quite often free. There are many organizations where you will find a mentor. Treat them to lunch or at the very least a coffee. When your mentor is an experienced business person, cultivate the relationship so they become a trusted, long-term connection.

A good business mentoring relationship provides the following benefits:

- A reduction in making incorrect business decisions.
- Important feedback in crucial areas, like communications, business relationships, and leadership skills.
- Knowledge of a variety of strategic business initiatives to take with your business.

Whether you find a mentor or hire a business coach, it's worth its weight in gold for the benefit of yours and your business development. A mentor will tell you what you need to hear, whereas your best friend may just tell you what you want to hear. A business coach is attentive to assisting you with general skills, whereas a mentor teaches you about specific circumstances. You can't get all this in one person.

Seminars, Networking & Professional Associations

Seminars or events are prescribed presentations by experts, which provide information and insights in shorter sound bites on how you might meet the ever-changing needs of your business. A seminar is usually a small group of people who actively participate in the learning of a particular subject matter. Seminars are held in hotel meeting spaces, at an academic institute or in a business conference room.

Why go to a seminar? A seminar may cover many topics of interest to you and your business. These topics might be business strategies, personal development, finance, marketing, creating your business plan, or how to pitch to investors. Or you use the seminar as a means to build your business contacts. Trade seminars provide the opportunity to find new vendors. You receive a lot of education from many experts in a short period of time. New ideas, new people, away from your business are just what you need to feel inspired, motivated, and recharged to innovate in your business.

"An organization's ability to learn, and translate that learning into action rapidly, is the ultimate competitive advantage."
Jack Welch

You're motivated by hearing how the seminar speakers have changed their business to make it successful. You're inspired to try something new in your business. You have the ability to meet future clients face to face, which has a much greater impact than communicating by phone or email. You're able to hear about the latest industry trends, which helps you to stay ahead of your competition. A seminar is an investment in yourself and your business.

Business networking is an effective, inexpensive way to find things you require for your business through referrals and introductions. By growing your circle of influence and developing long-term connections, you create mutual opportunities to benefit everyone involved. Some of the benefits are increasing sales from referrals, learning new ideas to grow and manage your business, and finding new vendors. Networking is for giving, receiving ideas, and knowledge.

Many different types of opportunities show up when you network, so keep your ears and eyes open as you want to seize them when they appear. You build new connections, become more visible and increase your self-confidence. The relationships you build through networking can be a catalyst for your success as people like to do business with those they know and trust. Serving as a resource and helping others in your network to succeed will do wonders for you to be seen as the go-to person.

Networking is a key marketing campaign strategy to get your face and your business message in front of the same people over and over again. Who do people think of first when they need a product and/or service you deliver? Why, they will call you because you made yourself known. Follow-up is important to continue those great relationships you just created. Be selective about which networking events you go to. You want to find networking events which attract the people you want to meet. Many of these events have expert speakers in areas of interest either to your business or to your target market.

A professional association seeks to further a particular profession, uphold professional standards, and improve the profession through learning and research. Some member benefits might be:

- Access to a members-only section on the association's website.
- Updating your knowledge through conferences, seminars, workshops, and online education.
- Access to industry specific publications.
- Prospects for support from more senior members.
- Committees with political influence and resources.
- Association activities in civic and philanthropic ventures.

I've used many of these ideas to help me on my business journey. I returned to school two times after I left high school to get degrees to help me in my business life. I belong to several professional associations. I belong to networking groups like eWomen Network, the Premier Women's Business Network in North America. I have coaches and mentors to help me achieve my vision. I've taken many certificate courses at local colleges or online to upgrade specific skills. I attend lots of seminars so I learn from the best. If I can do it, so can you.

Knowledge Management

I showed you some ways to obtain knowledge outside your business. Did you know your business has an extensive array of knowledge available through your clients, your employees, your vendors and your business information? How do you use this knowledge to benefit your business? Having a knowledge strategy helps you manage your business. There are three important reasons to manage your business knowledge: it enables making good decisions, it makes learning a standard, and it inspires innovation and change in your business.

You may not be aware of all the places where significant and valuable knowledge exists in your business. It lives in your documents, in your ideas for innovation, in your existing business processes, or in your products and/or services design. You want to find and use this knowledge in a comprehensible and creative way. Knowledge management encourages a united process for recognizing, assessing, recovering, and distributing your business information. The resources may be information databases, your business documents, policies, procedures, and your employees' skills and experiences.

Have you done any market research for your business? Market research is used to target clients and the products and/or services they need. The information you keep on your clients and your vendors is a gold mine when you want to create new products and/or services or to improve the ones you already have. When you hire your employees; hire the most knowledgeable ones. Ensure you extract valuable knowledge from these employees by documenting and cross-training.

Keep abreast of changes or developments in global economics and politics, technology, environment and society, and how they touch and influence the business world. Join professional and trade associations to have access to their knowledge through publications and training. Go to seminars and conferences to see what are the newest innovations in your industry. These are just a few ideas; get creative and seek knowledge for your business so you have a knowledge advantage.

"Knowledge is power."
Sir Francis Bacon

Ok, you now know a few ways to gain knowledge for your business, but you also need to create a strategy for finding knowledge, synthesizing knowledge, and providing knowledge across your business. A strategy or plan is a set of procedures you apply across your business. Encourage your employees to commit to your knowledge plan. Inform them of all the benefits to your business. Appoint one or two employees as your business knowledge expert in your business.

Look at how effectively you're using your business knowledge currently to help you make your knowledge plan. Look at your business processes for finding and providing the knowledge. Do you have successful processes in place so your employees have everything they need for a knowledge plan?

This is an ongoing, living plan, just like your other business strategies are. There are financial benefits to your business knowledge. Use your business knowledge to develop new products and/or services or sell or license it for other businesses to use or use it to help you to have a larger share of the marketplace.

After creating your business knowledge strategy, you may require systems or tools to help you find and use your business knowledge. There are a variety of systems or tools to use, some of which are complicated and onerous to run. Look for something, which fits with your business and helps to solve issues, and won't bring you more issues to cope with. Find a system to manage your business activities and contribute to making business decisions. Your business functions more competently by using a variety of knowledge systems to interact with your clients, to limit your expenses, and to generate revenue.

A knowledge management system is any system which finds, keeps and recovers your business knowledge information, advances teamwork, finds knowledge sources, mines sources for concealed knowledge, and uses your business knowledge to enhance your business.

Using Knowledge in Your Business

Good, you have a knowledge strategy in place. Let's look at how you use this knowledge in your business. Your business information is organized data and knowledge is the power to use what you know. There are two types of business knowledge, obvious and implied. Obvious knowledge is information that is found in a database or a book or is your policies and procedures. Implied knowledge is when you know details which are often learned from your experience such as a salesman who doesn't give you a great deal until you participate in his favourite charity golf tourney.

People, processes, and technology all help to implement your knowledge strategy. It's important to ensure your business knowledge is easily shared amongst your employees and doesn't disappear when an employee gets sick or leaves or goes on vacation. Making knowledge sharing a part of your business culture makes it more comfortable and normal for your employees to share. Create a collaborative culture where they understand sharing their knowledge helps them be more effective in their roles. Make knowledge sharing part of your employee performance review. Start first with your employees close to retirement age. You don't want them leaving without first capturing what's in their heads. The same is true for contract employees.

You want to identify the processes to capture, extract, validate, store, and use your business knowledge. Technology helps to support these processes and aids in finding the knowledge no matter where it lives. Whatever system you choose, make sure it's easy to implement and to use.

"There is no wealth like knowledge,
and no poverty like ignorance."
Buddha

You want to have agreements with your employees to keep your business knowledge confidential, to limit your employees from working for the competition when they leave your business, or to limit them from creating a competing business and stealing your clients. There are many ways to get employee buy-in. Offer incentives to employees for finding ways to improve your business processes or innovations to your products and/or services. Some other ideas are to hold brainstorming sessions, create a knowledge repository, have a knowledge champion, cross train your employees, adopt the practice of duplicate and replicate – don't reinvent the wheel. Training is an important method for dispersing important knowledge, skills, and best practices throughout your business.

Using knowledge may help you reduce the time you deliver a quote, proposal or product and/or service to your clients. This makes you highly poised to succeed. As you grow your business, you're able to consistently improve your results when you apply your knowledge management strategy across your business. When you have, processes established for describing, sharing, and repeating, your business takes advantage of its learning to solve business problems. Generating new knowledge through efficient knowledge sharing, teamwork, and information distribution inspires innovation.

Having the ability to identify emerging market trends might be very advantageous so you're offering new and innovative products and/or services to your marketplace before your competition. You have an upswing in your client satisfaction rates because you have an improved understanding of their needs from your client feedback. When you have an increased knowledge of what your clients want, you have the opportunity to improve the quality of your vendors. Your employees' productivity improves as they have access to knowing the best ways to accomplish tasks from their co-workers.

You've just learned about the knowledge in your business, how to have a strategy or plan to use knowledge, and how to apply knowledge in your business. Remember, for your business knowledge to make a transformation in your business, you need to communicate its importance, how are you using it, and you must lead by example. When you follow these guidelines, it's a big differentiator for your business.

Next is the money journey; it's all about the **Money**, how much you spend, and how much you make.

CHAPTER 9

WHERE'S THE $$MONEY$$?

ೞೞೞೞೞೞೞೞೞೞ

Banking & Credit

One of the most important pieces of your business is the money. When you first start your business, it's best to get a business bank account. It's crucial to keep your personal money separate from your business money.

A business bank account is essential to track the money going in and going out of your business. Government revenue agencies really don't like it when you mix business money with personal money. Mixing your personal and business money becomes messy and you don't have a clear audit trail. A business bank account is an asset to your business.

A business bank account gives your business credibility. It shows you're serious about your company being a business and not just a hobby. You're indicating you're a professional. This puts you in a favourable light with your clients, employees, and vendors. Another significant reason for keeping your business money separate is to protect your personal assets. This is important if you're sued or you can't pay your business debts. Having a business bank account to use for your business expenses ensures your business is a separate entity.

You want to create a relationship with the institution where you have your business bank account. Make an appointment with the branch manager to develop this relationship. It helps you when you need financial help. Your financial institution is also a strong networking resource for your business. Your business representative helps you learn best practices to manage your money and put your business in the best light when you want extra financial help.

Corporate banking offers a wide range of products and services to help many types of businesses. Do your homework and shop around to find the best deal for your business. Look for a financial institution who understands your business type, your business transactions, and your cash deposit needs. Your fees are a legitimate business expense, but look around as there is a variation in fees and benefits at different types of financial institutions.

You want to establish credit for your business early. You don't want your business credit to be tied to your personal credit; it lowers your score and you look over-leveraged. Your business credit score is a different number than your personal score. There are many ways to affect your credit score, like paying your bills on time, how much available credit you have with credit cards, and lines of credit, how long you have had a credit profile, the number of times an inquiry is made to your credit profile, etc.

Establish your business with business credit bureaus such as Dun & Bradstreet or Equifax or Trans Union. List a dedicated telephone number and business address in places like your local Yellow Pages or online. To get rated you need to build credit. How do you this? Look for vendors to provide you with business accounts, like Office Depot or Staples. Approach vendors you're already doing business with, like your lawyer or your accountant, to ask if they will report your business credit history to the business credit bureau. When you need equipment for your business, look at leasing as this helps to grow your credit. Your business requires a business plan, business credit history, and a good relationship with your financial institution. Start small and work your way up. It's better to get approved for the credit before you need it.

> "A bank is a place that will lend you money
> if you can prove that you don't need it."
> Bob Hope

With a great credit score, you negotiate better payment terms with vendors, and limit the number of times you use cash for products and/or services. A great credit score allows you to negotiate better credit terms and interest rates from financial institutions and lenders. You also increase the value of your business when you want to sell it in the future. Watch your credit-utilization ratio; this a ratio of the amount of credit your business owes and the amount of credit available to your business. Be aware a high credit-utilization ratio adversely affects your business credit score.

Cash Flow & Profitability

Your cash flow is the movement of money in and out of your business. It's best to track this with a cash flow statement. There are two kinds of cash flows, positive and negative. A positive cash flow is when more money is coming into your business than is going out of your business. A negative cash flow is when there is more money going out of your business than is coming into your business. Manage your cash flow efficiently so you aren't in a negative cash flow state. I prefer to have a budget to show me what monies I expect to come in during the month and a list of all the bills I have to pay.

Having a budget governs what you're doing with your monthly cash. This way at any given moment during the month, you balance your budget against your actual cash flow to know exactly where you stand. The life force of your business is cash. When you learn to do a cash flow analysis every month or even bi-monthly, which is my preference, you have a much easier time growing your business without creating a deficit and a crisis for you to manage.

Managing your cash flow wisely has a huge impact on your business success. When you have a positive cash flow, you're able to pay employees, purchase products and/or services you require, and pay yourself. When you don't manage your cash flow, by spending too much or not paying attention to what you're spending it on, you're inviting business failure.

There are several reasons why your business has cash flow issues, but most of them boil down to a lack of management and making poor decisions. Another thing to remember is large amounts of cash don't translate to large amounts of profit and, vice versa, large amounts of profit don't translate into large amounts of cash.

> *"When it comes to money, ignorance is NOT bliss.*
> *What you don't know CAN hurt you."*
> Sandra S. Simmons, Unleash Your Cash Flow Mojo:
> The Business Owner's Guide to Predicting,
> Planning and Controlling Your Company's Cash Flow

One of the first priorities in your business is profitability. Profit is what's left from your business revenue after you have paid all your business expenses. Profitability determines how successful your business is. How do you have a profitable business? By being the best in your business marketplace and keeping your clients happy. When investors see a return on their investment, they will be interested in funding your business.

Profitability is your primary business focus. Delegate the day-to-day operations of your business so you focus your attention on managing your business growth and its finances. Give yourself a salary from day one. Make and stick to a business budget. To understand how to increase your profitability, you want to keep a close eye on which financial strategies are working and which ones aren't working.

It's essential, right at the beginning of your business, to focus on being profitable. Your initial profitability requires market growth and sales. Once you're out of the startup phase, focus on opportunities for growth. In your startup phase, you work to gain a loyal client following and attract new business by referrals. Your profits may be lower initially as your business builds its reputation.

While your business needs to make a profit to ensure its survival, you must have the correct technologies, employees, products and/or services with fair market pricing in place, otherwise you find yourself chasing your business profits just like the elusive pot of gold at the end of the rainbow.

Some important measures of success are profits, positive cash flow, controllable debts, with always an eye to finding and maintaining your business efficiencies.

Bookkeeping & Accounting

It's important to accurately track your cash flow, expenses, and all the financial transactions for your business. Bookkeeping is the day-to-day record keeping for your finances. Record every transaction, whether it's a sale or a purchase. This is an important function in your business foundation.

Keeping track of your business financial transactions by collecting your invoices and receipts in a shoebox isn't an efficient way to manage these transactions. I worked for a major film producer where each movie had its own set of books. The production managers used to bring me a mess of paper in a box. It took days to sort it out before I even began to enter the transactions in an organized fashion to give to the accountant. It was a major headache.

Hire a bookkeeper when you aren't willing or able to record your business financial transactions in a logical system as they occur. An accomplished bookkeeper creates financial accounts to give your business true information about its financial actions. These accounts are key to the future success of your business. A good bookkeeper can:

- Regularly record your business financial transactions.
- Generate client invoices.
- Reconcile your bank statements.
- Write checks for you to sign.
- Maintain and balance your ledgers or books.
- Process your payroll.
- Prepare reports.
- Keep your financial documentation organized.
- Understand your business.
- Keep you apprised of any issues they see.

The other financial professional important to your business is an accountant. An accountant helps you understand the terminology and how to manage your business finances. With an accountant's assistance, you start your business on the right path.

"Science is much easier than Accounting."
K.C. Tshwaane

Accounting lets you track your business assets, liabilities, and income. This allows you to make smart, knowledgeable business decisions based on your past business performance and the current financial state of your business. You grow your business in a managed way. An accountant can:

- Help you with your business plan.
- Implement your business accounting system.
- Make sure you pay the appropriate business taxes.
- Advise you on your business financial decisions.

- Handle an audit when your business has one.
- Create your yearly business financial statements.
- Help you understand your business financial statements.
- Analyze your business data for growth and profitability opportunities.
- Understand changing laws and regulations and how they apply to your business.

An accountant helps you see the big picture when you're standing in the weeds. They see the financial information from many different businesses and industries. They see not only the best practices of these businesses; they also see the mistakes. They give you valuable advice to save you many headaches.

> *"A firm's income statement may be, likened to a bikini-what it reveals is interesting but what it conceals is vital."*
> Burton G. Malkiel

Receivables & Payables

Accounts Receivables are the money your business receives for providing your clients with your products and/or services. When you deliver your products and/or services and until your client pays, the amount owing is considered your Accounts Receivable and for your client, it's an Accounts Payable. The receivable is listed as an asset on your business balance sheet.

You need to decide how much credit you allow a client. Establish your credit allowance based on the client's finances and their payment history with you. Be vigilant and reduce credit limits when your client shows they have difficulty in paying. Ask a new client to pay with a credit card before you deliver any products and/or services when you're not sure of their ability to pay.

When your receivables are too high, it means you're not doing a good job of collecting the money owed to you. This puts your business at risk. You may not have the necessary cash flow to pay your bills. On the other hand, when your receivables are too low, it means you didn't make any sales or you're not offering competitive payment terms.

There will sometimes be receivables you cannot collect. These aren't considered an asset to your business. When you have clients, who don't pay you on time or don't pay you at all, you need to get the money up-front before you deliver your products and/or services. Sometime you have to sell the receivables for pennies on the dollar to a collection agency. In some cases, you use your receivables as collateral for a loan.

I once worked with a business where the owner sold firewood on the side. When I arrived, there was an outstanding number of receivables worth several thousand dollars. Two of these accounts were on his books from the previous year. I started to contact everyone and was successful in collecting the amounts owed. Except for one gentleman who decided to hide behind the fact he used the business he worked for to complete the deal. There was one problem with this; the firewood was for his home use, not for use by the company.

I phoned the president and explained the situation. I didn't believe it was right for an executive at his business to be using the business to purchase an item for personal use and then not pay for it. The outstanding bill was paid right after my phone call. Because of my tenacity, the owner had all his outstanding monies collected. Sometimes you have to think outside of the standard norms to find a solution.

Accounts Payables are the money your business owes for buying products and/or services from your vendors. When you receive your products and/or services and you pay for them, the amount owing is considered your Accounts Payable and for your vendor, it's an Accounts Receivable. The payable is listed as a liability on your business balance sheet.

One of the places where you experience employee fraud is in payables. You need to have good controls to prevent this abuse. I advise my clients to segregate the responsibilities by having one role to process the payments and generate the cheques and another, usually more senior role, to review and sign your cheques. Better still, require two signatures on the cheques. You need to be vigilant for fraudulent invoicing.

The task of segregating job functions is really easy to setup in accounting software. You're limiting each employee so no one, not even you, processes a payment and generates a signed cheque. I hear of many sad stories from businesses where they trusted an employee, only to be robbed by them to the detriment of their business. I suggest you use police background checks and credit checks before you hire any employee to work with your business monies.

Government & Taxes

When setting up your business, you choose the appropriate business type. Next, you register your business with the government. This starts your relationship with the government.

Learn what regulations and laws apply to your business. The regulations and laws set the rules and standards to ensure the business marketplace is consistent, fair, and safe for everyone who participates. You may need to know the rules at many levels of government depending on the products and/or services you offer and where your business is registered and/or located.

> *"Government's view of the economy could be summed up in a few short phrases: If it moves, tax it. If it keeps moving, regulate it. And if it stops moving, subsidize it."*
> Ronald Reagan

Many of these laws are to protect both you, your business, your clients, your employees, and your vendors from wrongdoing or illegal activities. They have a tendency to fall into the following types:

Labour laws apply to how your business interacts with your employees. Labour laws cover things like minimum wage, worker protection, hours worked, vacation time and pay, public holidays, leaves of absence, and termination.

Regulatory laws apply standards affecting how your business operates in certain circumstances. Regulatory laws cover areas like building, environment, global trade, and licensing.

Reporting laws apply to how your business reports its finances to any investors and the government. These laws require you to keep your business activities transparent which helps to prevent misconduct and fraud.

Tax laws apply to how your business reports its financial picture to the government. Reporting your business income and expenses determines how much and to what level of government you owe taxes. There are also taxes to be paid on your sales, depending on where you're located. Your taxes need to be remitted regularly as required by the government you owe them to.

Your taxes may be filed differently depending on the type of business you created and where your business is located. Many countries have tax laws that impose a tax on your business income. You're taxed by the country you're doing business in. It's your responsibility to know the rules. Your accountant is a trusted advisor on your taxes. You have to report both your business income and business expenses.

When you don't file, and pay your taxes, what happens to you and your business isn't very nice. Don't ignore your tax responsibilities. This is a bad decision for many reasons. You hurt your business credit when you fail to pay your taxes. You pay a penalty for not filing or for not paying. You're charged interest on the amounts owing until you do pay.

There are steps you take when for some reason you don't have the funds to pay the taxes. You can negotiate to set-up a payment plan. You may be in a financial mess, but it's your responsibility to clean it up. Get the help of a tax professional to help you when you have many years of unpaid taxes. You don't want the government to take legal action against you; they have more money than you, which means they usually win their case.

The importance of paying your taxes isn't just to keep your business in good standing. The monies collected are used by governments to fund public services. There are fewer funds for important services which might include health care, child care, or infrastructure projects when you don't pay your share. Your country's quality of life is supported by the taxes you and your business pay.

Different Types of Funding

There may be times you want to have an injection of cash to help your business grow. It's a wise idea to know what kinds of funding might be available to you when you need it. There are basically two ways to fund your business; one is debt and the other is equity.

When you use debt, you have to repay the funds within a specified time period and usually with a specified amount of interest. However, you retain complete ownership of your business. When you use equity, you're giving an investor a share in your business in exchange for their cash. You won't have to repay the cash to the investor. However, your business isn't solely yours and you may have to share control.

Over the course of your business life you may have funding from different places. There are different criteria to meet for different types of funding options. It depends on your business model and how well you sell yourself and your business. Be positive, flexible, and vigilant in your efforts when you're looking for funding.

"An entrepreneur without funding is a musician without an instrument."
Robert A. Rice Jr.

Some of the different types of funding are:

Bootstrapping comes from reinvesting the money your business makes back into the business.

Self-funding is funding your business from your savings or personal debt such as your credit cards.

Friends and/or Family is money raised by your friends and/or family. Be careful about giving equity to your friends and/or family as this can backfire, especially if your business fails.

Angel Investors are wealthy people willing to invest in your business. Sometimes they're an investment group which shares the risk.

Cloud Funding is via a group which allows you to pitch to investors over the internet. When your pitch is successful, there are multiple investors. Make sure you understand the cloud operator's restrictions.

Partners means you take on a partner which is strategic when you align your business resources such as a property maintenance business partnering with a property management business.

Venture Capital is usually sought after in the early stages of your business, but be warned they want a significant share of your business in return for a large investment – quite often this is a controlling share.

Business Loans are obtained from financial institutions. You need a good business plan, profitable financial projections, and your own money. These take time to get, but you retain business ownership.

Crowd Funding is found on the internet and allows you to reach large numbers of potential investors. You create a community around your product including users to test, use, and help to innovate.

Advance Orders are about raising money through pre-sales. This works well when you already have clients who want what you're selling. It's a great way to authenticate your business ideas.

Grants are from non-profits and government programs.

Home Equity Loans are given to you using the equity you have in your home.

Corporate Sponsors help you when you're able to offer something of value they want.

I am now at the end of providing you with an understanding of money and your business. The last thing I want to discuss is the **Framework** you require for a solid foundation for your business.

CHAPTER 10

CREATE YOUR BUSINESS FRAMEWORK

ശയശഇശഇശയശഇശഇശഇ

Your Business Plan

A business plan is the roadmap to your business vision. Your business goals and your plans for obtaining them are documented in your business plan. A business plan is a valuable asset, whether you're starting a business, have an existing business, want to grow your business, or you want to leave your business.

Your business plan isn't just for business funding; it's the blueprint to how your business operates. It helps you get clear on what you want to do to have a successful business. It ensures you won't miss any required steps and identifies potential issues by looking at the big picture.

Your business plan is a living document. Review it at least annually. Keep copies of all versions of your business plan as it provides you with a history to know how well you met your targets. Your business plan is a résumé for your business. It defines your business purpose, vision, goals, operations, and finances. Use your business plan to share your objectives with your employees, your vendors, and potential investors.

This is what I like to put in a business plan:

- **Business Overview:** Your mission, your vision, your values, your goals, your priorities, your objectives, your products and/or services, your unique features, and your opportunity.
- **Business Environment:** An examination of your clients, competition, marketplace, and industry; how you measure up against these and how you differentiate your business.
- **Business Description:** Your unique advantage over the competition. How you differentiate your business by your delivery, finances, management, marketing, operations, technology, sales, staffing, and client service.
- **Business Strategy:** Your future blueprint, how you plan to grow, what opportunities are you poised to seize, how will you avoid risks, how will you market your business, and what is your exit strategy.
- **Financial Assessment**: Your finances as prepared by your accountant and include your balance sheet, budget, cash flow and income statements, and profit forecasts.

- **Action Plan**: what steps you take to put your business plan into action to meet your business goals and objectives.
- **Appendix:** include supporting documentation like bank statements, appraisals, insurance, agreements, research, etc.

"If you're trying to create a company, it's like baking a cake.
You have to have all the ingredients in the right proportion."
Elon Musk

There are some common mistakes to avoid:

- Not having a business plan.
- Not knowing the purpose of your business plan.
- Not having a well-defined business model.
- Not doing your research.
- Not paying attention to the realities of the marketplace.
- Not preparing your finances.
- Not using your business plan to guide your business.

Your business plan is a tool to describe and clarify your business' operations, goals, and strategies. The notable areas of your business are covered in your business plan.

Build Your Team

Your "A" team includes:

1. A **Virtual Assistant** or **Business Manager** – previously known as a right hand.
2. An **Accountant** to prepare your books, your financial statements, your year-end closure, and your taxes.
3. A **Banker** to provide you with financial advice and help you to leverage OTM (Other People's Money).
4. A **Lawyer** to manage all your legal affairs – no one likes to be sued.
5. A **Marketing Professional** to help you engage with existing and new clients, your branding, and how you get your message out to the world.
6. A **Sales Professional** to help you target your clients, develop

your product and/or service offerings, pricing, and sell to your clients.

7. An **IT Specialist** to manage all your automation and database requirements.

8. An **Insurance Broker** to protect your business assets.

9. And last but not least, your **Business Coach** or **Mentor**, your confidant, your best friend.

A good **Virtual Assistant** or **Business Manager** represents a major resource in a small business. This is your right hand. You have a huge return on your investment, when you take the time and make an effort to nurture this relationship. Why? Because when your employees feel heard, seen, appreciated, and respected they're more engaged in your business. An engaged employee is more than likely to bend over backwards to provide excellent value. Content employees want to satisfy your clients; they want to do a good job, and they want to stay in the job.

Why is this important to you? Because it means you're consistently providing exceptional client service, which is good for your business and its growth. It also means you aren't losing money on employee replacement, retraining, and the unavoidable rookie blunders of new hires. Another benefit to you is a trusted employee who minds the store when you have other important activities you must do to develop your business so you keep your cash register ringing. You cannot be a Jack or Jill of all Trades and grow a successful, profitable business.

An **Accountant** makes sure you don't get into trouble with your taxes. They give you financial reports which are beneficial in your business dealings with your banker or other potential investors. You will know at all times what your financial picture looks like – how much money is coming into your business and how much money is going out of your business.

A **Banker** not only helps you set up your business banking, but is there when you're looking for money to help your business grow. A banker who knows you and your particular situation is better equipped to help you when you need it.

A **Lawyer** manages all your legal affairs; to make sure your contracts are protecting you, your business, and your clients. One lawsuit might cost you the business you worked so hard to build.

An **Insurance Broker** advises you on what insurance you require to protect your business assets.

A **Marketing Professional** creates a marketing plan to target your market, help to optimize your media messaging, look after your branding, and find out what your competition is doing.

A **Sales Professional** creates a sales plan to identify how you target your sales activities, where you go to network, where you find leads, how many touches a client requires in your sales cycle, and how to educate your clients on the benefits and the expected results from using your products and/or services.

An **IT Specialist** understands the constantly changing technology landscape. They advise you on systems, help you analyse your business, and suggest ways for you to be more streamlined and efficient. This allows you to be more competitive in the financial, administrative, and operational areas of your business and able to scale as your business grows.

A **Business Coach or Mentor** listens to your ideas, guides you, keeps you accountable, and tells you the truth you cannot find for yourself. They provide the vision, the tools, the systems, and the effective strategies to help you develop and improve your business in ways you might overlook or not even think of. You want to thrive in your business, not just survive. A good business coach or mentor helps you with both transactional and transformational actions. The bottom line is, you want your business to benefit your clients, to make money, to be profitable, and to achieve success.

"Great things in business are never done by one person.
They're done by a team of people."
Steve Jobs

You want to climb the mountain and shout from the top:
"I Did It – I'm Successful!"

Here's an example of how a team adjusted to make the most of a project by utilizing the team members' skill sets efficiently.

I was working for my client, a Canadian bank, on a project to automate the workflow in their Wealth Management division by creating a single sign-on application dashboard for securities transactions. It was a very small team with four programmers, the Project Manager (PM), the Quality Analyst (QA), and myself as the Business Analyst (BA). When I arrived, the project was already underway with one of the modules completed. The project structure had been created; however, I was a catalyst for three significant changes to the project workflow.

Because I have skills as a Graphical User Interface (GUI) programmer, the PM and I decided it saved time if I coded the GUI, rather than just creating wireframes. This saved development time. The development team expressed concerns with the lack of input from business users during the product development phase. Realizing a liaison person was required as an effective conduit for communication between the business users and the development team, I took the initiative to request I be involved in the technical discussions to round out the expertise and have a direct conduit to the business. As a result, there was a more efficient analysis done before the development work started, which resulted in less changes being requested by the user group during the UAT phase.

The Business Director, the PM and I also decided I'd create and conduct all user training. This reduced the amount of support calls after a new module was rolled out. Additionally, it allowed the programmers to devote more time to the actual development work, thereby reducing the project timeline. I enjoyed working with this group and brainstorming to solve the technical challenges.

By looking at all the skill sets I brought to the table, this team was able to devise a new more effective and efficient workflow and the project delivered a better solution in a shorter timeframe.

Standard Operating Procedures

Before I talk about Standard Operating Procedures (SOPs), I want to ensure you understand what a repeatable process is, and why you need them in your business. A repeatable process is a set of activities that are easily repeated. Performing activities over and over again doesn't mean you have a repeatable process with an expected result. A repeatable process is the capability to complete an activity to produce an outcome an unlimited number of times with an expected level of quality. Document your business process so anyone who performs the process achieves the same predictable results over and over again. You want to condense the work in your business to the smallest and most valued actions.

Why do you want to have repeatable processes in your business? Because they:

- Make each part of your business process a clear objective.
- Provide the steps logically and sequentially.
- Reduce the number of business decisions you make.
- Increase your efficiencies and productivity.
- Provide uniformity throughout your business.
- Create the ability to measure and track your business outputs.

Begin designing your process with the end result in mind and work back to the beginning. Test your process so you know it produces the exact same result each time. To be efficient, only include the steps you absolutely need to accomplish your desired end result. As you repeat the process over and over again, the person or the system performing the process builds a history of experience that helps to increase your efficiencies and improves your business productivity. To have a repeatable process someone follows, document the process so it's followed exactly the same way each time.

"If you can't describe what you are doing as a process,
you don't know what you're doing."
W. Edwards Deming

SOPS are your documented business processes to ensure your products and/or services are provided consistently to your clients' every time. When you started your business, you, as the fearless leader made all the major decisions. As your company grows, you aren't able to make all the decisions anymore. Documenting your SOPs helps you to grow more easily and to continue to **WOW** your clients, your employees, and your vendors constantly.

When writing your SOPs, answer the following questions:

- Who is the actor – what is the job role or person accountable?
- What are the activities they perform?
- What is the expected result of the performed activities?
- Is this written in the simplest terms?

Some business areas to benefit from SOPs are administration, finance, human resources, marketing, payroll, operations, sales, and information technology. Tie your SOPs to your performance reviews where you have each employee responsible for keeping them up-to-date. Use them to create training manuals for use with new hires. By creating SOPs, you have blueprinted your business.

Next I will explore how a business blueprint helps you to be more streamlined and efficient. A business blueprint gives you peace of mind, enables you to be proactive and not reactive, and to provide WOW experiences to your clients, your employees, and your vendors. You sleep at night; you have work-life balance.

Blueprint Your Business

How does having a business model or blueprint of your actual current business state help you? It gives you a big-picture view of your business and why your business processes perform the way you have prescribed them to. A business blueprint helps to clarify your vision, your values, your goals, and your priorities so you know where you want to go with your business. A business blueprint allows you to get specific about your business so you see the big picture.

Your business blueprint has textual and numerical attributes and includes:

Your Business Identity is your brand, your vision, your target market and what are your differentiators, your business culture which includes your values, your workplace rules, and your behaviour expectations.

Your business identity enables you and others to understand how your business is making a noticeable difference in the world.

Your Business Strategy is your goals and your priorities and how you meet these, the timeframe for achieving your goals, the resources you use, and any performance metrics you measure.

Your Business Assets are your products and/or services, your organizational model, including roles and responsibilities, finances, intellectual property, sales distribution channels, and any physical assets like equipment, real estate, technology, etc. Make sure you include your products and/or services in your business blueprint as they solve problems for your clients.

Your External Business Environment is your clients, your vendors, any partners, competitors, market and industry demographics, compliance, new technologies, and general business trends. Your clients are the people you want to work with and the people who most benefit from your products and/or services.

> *"By failing to prepare, you are preparing to fail."*
> Benjamin Franklin

Some of the questions to ask when gathering requirements for your business blueprint are:

- Who are your target clients?
- What client problems or challenges do you solve?
- What value do you deliver?
- How do you reach, acquire, and keep your clients?
- How do you define and differentiate your products and/or services?
- How do you generate revenue?
- What's your cost structure?
- What's your profit margin?

Your business blueprint will be unique to your business. It tells the story of what your business is and what its objectives are. Your business blueprint provides you with a 360-degree view of your business to provide the foundation for a predictive, justifiable business plan for handling challenges and opportunities for growth and success.

When you implement your business blueprint, you prioritize and guide your business performance and growth. New ideas, new strategies, and new tools are an essential part of what you need to survive the changes in today's business climate. The marketplace today is very volatile and you're better able to recognize challenges and to identify the strategies you need to implement to manage them. Having a blueprint of your business means when you need to change, you know exactly what areas of your business you have to apply the changes to.

Automate Your Systems

Your business is structured, you have a blueprint, and your SOPs are in place. What more can you do to help your business? Automate your manual systems to have more time to **WOW** your clients, your employees, and your vendors. Today's businesses face extreme competition. Automation helps you to be competitive.

You want your business to be profitable. You don't want to be working in your business, you want to be working on your business. Automation allows you to grow smartly. When you don't grow your business, someone else will come along and take your place in the marketplace. While your business has important, but laborious activities requiring completion, not all of them are income-generating activities. If time is money, you need all the time you can get. Automation get you more time.

In a typical business day, there are so many activities to attend to: emails, phone calls, meetings, approvals, reports, follow-up, and tracking to name just a few. These are foundational activities to allow your business to run, but they take your time. This is time better spent on activities to make your cash register ring.

Avoid keeping up-to-date with technology at your own risk. Use technology to help you open new markets, serve your clients, increase efficiencies, and create new products and/or services, which gives you a fighting chance of staying ahead of your competition. Automate the easiest processes first, build a business culture to embrace automation, and start small by focusing on one business activity.

> *"The first rule of any technology used in a business is that automation applied to an efficient operation will magnify the efficiency. The second is that automation applied to an inefficient operation will magnify the inefficiency."*
> Bill Gates

Reasons to automate your business:

- **Stay Competitive** to get more profit from your business.
- **Reduce Errors** to help identify and eliminate errors.
- **Increase Production Speed** to enable activities to be completed in shorter timeframes.
- **Increase Productivity** so more jobs completed, shorter delivery times, and optimized operations.
- **Eliminate Steps** to optimize efficiencies on repeatable activities.
- **Improve Quality** by having accurate information at every step.
- **Remove the Human Component** to eliminate common and repetitive activities.
- **Use Less Employee Time** for routine business activities.
- **Save Money** because it takes less time, less errors, and less rework.

Automating your business activities reduces costs associated with inefficiencies and errors. Payments for products never received, slow approvals for sales, and late payments are all expensive errors you don't want in your business.

After automating a business activity, make sure it's working perfectly. The data collected over time is used to find insights into your business. Learn if the automated activity is making your employees lives easier or more difficult. It's easy to automate marketing, contacts, sales, follow-up, inventory, social media, client support, testimonial requests, lunches or catering, passwords, employee scheduling, etc.

There's no end to the type of activities you will automate today, however, you still need a person to oversee everything, to monitor, and to make sure everything runs smoothly. Get started today to find the benefits of automation in your business. When necessary, outsource the work. You want to have more time for focusing on the things you do best in your business to make your cash register ring.

Remember: **Your Time = Your Money**

Get Organized to Execute

This is the last item I want to talk about. Organizing your business is a daunting task, but it's doable.

Your business plan is your blueprint to run your business. It's helpful to create your business plan before you open your business, but you can create one after you've started as it will help you get focused on where to place your effort. You want to cover your business operations, including employees, budgets, sales and marketing, and production if you have products and financial projections.

> *"An organization's ability to learn, and translate that learning into action rapidly, is the ultimate competitive advantage."*
> Jack Welch

Spend some time creating your business plan. Get advice from others who have experience in your industry. Once you finalize your plan, be prepared to follow your plan. Remember, your plan is a living document; review it at least yearly, if not quarterly, and make updates as you innovate your business. It's also a useful tool when you're looking for cash injections to your business. You share it with potential lenders, investors, or partners.

> *"It takes as much energy to wish as it does to plan."*
> Eleanor Roosevelt

To be successful in business, you need to be organized. Being organized helps you to complete activities and stay on top of what needs to be completed. A point to note – your business activities don't exist as stand-alone activities, they interact with other activities in your business. When you change an activity, make it a point to look at the activities they intersect with. For instance, you don't want to be requiring the approval of a role that no longer exists.

Let's take a look at some items to help you be organized.

To-Do & Not-To-Do Lists - Create these every day at the end of your day to start first thing the next day. Prioritize your activities and schedule appointments for them. Make sure these aren't activities you can delegate; they must be activities only you can do to **Create CALM From Chaos**^{TM} in your business. As you complete them, mark them off your list. This ensures you don't forget something and you complete all the activities essential for your business to thrive.

Keep Detailed Records – Keep detailed records to know where you're at any given moment in time. You want to see both the big picture and the details to support it. This allows you to clearly see your successes and your challenges so you know where to focus your effort. All successful businesses keep detailed records. By keeping detailed records, you will know where the business stands financially and what potential challenges you're facing. Knowing your potential challenges gives you time to create strategies to overcome the obstacles that prevent you from being successful and growing your business.

Know Your Competition – Know your competition to be successful. You learn from what works for your completion and implement a version in your business or you learn what isn't working so you don't implement this in your business.

Understand Risks and Rewards – Take calculated actions in your business to make it grow. Know both the risk and the reward for the action. Create best case and worst case scenarios to look at the possibilities of taking different actions.

Be Creative – Always look for different ways to innovate and improve your business. You don't want to be in the sea of sameness, you want to stand out from your competition. Be open to new ideas and new ways to use in your business.

Stay Focused – Rome wasn't built in a day and neither will your business be. Don't be discouraged when you don't make any money when you first open. It takes time for clients to know you're open to serve them. Keep focused on your goals and letting the world know you're here.

Be Prepared to Make Sacrifices – At first, to get your business up and running, you may make sacrifices, you may not have time for your family or friends. Are you spending more time in your business than you do as an employee? Stay passionate to your dream. Believe in you. You make it happen.

Provide WOW Service – Many businesses don't provide **WOW** service to their clients. When you provide your clients with **WOW** experiences, you go a long way to create client loyalty and retention. Remember to do this for your employees and your vendors too. Make you and your business memorable.

Be Consistent – Create repeatable activities so you're providing consistency each time you perform. This is a key factor in being successful and making money.

Keep Meetings to a Minimum – Too many meetings have people hanging around who have very little to offer. Only meet with those who absolutely need to be there. Keep your meetings short and to the point.

Keep Email Messages to a Minimum – Too many people get messages they don't need. Send your email only to those who need to know or who need to take some kind of action.

Keep Policies and Procedures Current – At least once a year, review all your policies and procedures to see if they are current. If they aren't, bring them up-to-date or archive them.

Have an Exit Plan – Know what you need to do when you want to sell your business or close it down.

Next I want to talk about what is **Your Next Step** after reading and integrating all the knowledge I have provided in this book.

CHAPTER 11

YOUR NEXT STEP

I've taken you on a journey through your business. I've shown you a variety of ways to use to make your business more structured and systemized, which allows you to work smarter, not harder and to be a profitable success. I've provided you with tools to change your perspective and mindset so you have the clarity and focus required to run a successful business. I've given you many ways to **WOW** your clients, your employees, and your vendors. You want to have everyone on your team working synergistically to serve.

You're now able to bring **CALM** to your chaos. However, if you're still struggling after reading this book, please don't hesitate, walk, No, run as Fast as you can and connect with me so I can help you **Create CALM From Chaos**™ in your business. Find me at LaurieKGrant.com.

I wish you all the best on your business journey.

When you need help, please connect with me so my brilliance will light your way.

I'm the Premier International Business Strategy and Efficiency Expert, Award Winning and International Bestselling Author, Global Speaker, and Thought Leader. I'm the Founder and CEO of FutureWave Group, leading the day-to-day responsibilities, including client consultations, managing projects and everything in between.

I'm well qualified with a Bachelor of Arts degree in Information Technology with a minor in Technical and Professional Writing from York University, an Honours Diploma in Electronics Engineering Technology – Control Systems from Seneca College of Applied Arts and Technology, and Certificates in Effective Communications and Human Relations, Enterprise Analysis and Consulting Skills, and Organizational Change Management.

I've worked in a variety of industries and reinvented myself several times over the years. I had my first job at 16 and I dispatched couriers. I next went to restaurants and then bars where I worked with many West Coast bands. A move to Toronto, Ontario found opportunities in film, television, and video. My last role in the entertainment industry was Acquisitions Director, where I negotiated the rights to Grade B movies to turn into videos for distribution. I negotiated the music rights and worked with ad agencies to create box covers, one sheets, and posters for video stores. The firm went bankrupt. I went back to school in an old bus garage to learn about trades and technology. I chose technology as I have a unique ability to see patterns everywhere and most especially in any kind of **Chaos**. I see the big picture and find the unique solution to **Create CALM From Chaos**^{TM}.

I started my IT career working for EDS and ended at IBM. I have 20+ years global experience designing and implementing business transformation solutions for a variety of businesses including Fortune Top 50 corporations, multi-nationals, mid-sized businesses, start-ups, and government entities. Some of my clients have been organizations such as EDS, IBM, Blue Cross, Anheuser Busch, Enbridge Gas, various Canadian Federal and Provincial Ministries, RBC, CIBC, York University, Dow Jones, ADP, Funddata, Debi/Davidge, and General Motors to name a few.

I successfully bridge relationships with business users, technology designers, clients, and vendors. I expertly engage people with diverse views, values, and strengths to generate innovative and sustainable solutions to address the root causes of complex challenges within organizations. I am esteemed by my clients and colleagues for an unprecedented ability to assess any challenge at hand and generate the most innovative and sustainable solution. My expertise fosters thriving, profitable growth for the businesses I work with.

I'm the author of **Create CALM From Chaos** – 7 Steps To Maximize Power, Performance and Profits^{TM}. I support my clients to **Create CALM From Chaos**^{TM} to put their business on the correct track to success. My insights and savvy business skills help you see the future is now. My focus on the future is evident in this book which teaches you how to create and sustain **CALM** throughout the lifecycle of your business idea. I harness the power of clarity to reach optimal business success.

With FutureWave Group, I help my clients blueprint or model their business, create standard operating procedures to provide a solid foundation, find efficiencies, and create more profitable results by working smarter, not harder. I inspire my clients to find breakthrough strategies uniquely designed to work for them, to show them how to overcome business adversity no matter what it looks like, setting them on a business trajectory to financial abundance, personal freedom, and significant success.

May my brilliance light your way to success.

It's my passion to help you find the **CALM** in your Chaos by creating easy, sustainable systems so your business works for you. Let's have a conversation to see how we can bring **CALM** to your business. Go to BreakTheChaos.com to start the journey and in a few minutes, you'll be directed to my calendar to select a date and time to fit your schedule.

TESTIMONIALS

Laurie K. Grant is the person you want on your team. She rolls up her sleeves, dives right in, and gets to the root core of your business. Laurie provides a clear set of instructions for clarity in business formation or restructuring and has a proven track record of creating systems that achieve great success. **Sandra Yancey | CEO and Founder | eWomenNetwork, Inc., The Premier Women's Business Network in North America**

ᏣᏛᏬᏍᎠᏨᏓᏨᏣᏛᏬᏍᎠᏨ

Laurie K Grant has a savvy awareness of future trends in business. As a result, she was able to help me get clearly focused on my business. Where I was a loose cannon in organizational skills, she helped me start to compartmentalize my products in a way that made more sense, and therefore created more income for my company. **Carla Wynn Hall, President, The Soulful Pen**

ᏣᏛᏬᏍᎠᏨᏓᏨᏣᏛᏬᏍᎠᏨ

I've had the pleasure of knowing Laurie K. Grant for 10+ years, personally and professionally. She is a dedicated, driven professional, and with her vast experience, Laurie will make a great contribution to your bottom-line. Laurie not only identifies your needs; she takes them to the next level. She provides growth strategies, manages projects, builds long term relationships, and creates partnerships that will profit both your company and your clients. My advice: If you're looking to grow your existing business and create new opportunities, speak to Laurie K. Grant! **Brian Talbot, Account Director, Cofomo and Director of Business Development / Recruitment. Private Sector / Public Sector, Applied Technology Solutions(Global) Inc.**

ᏣᏛᏬᏍᎠᏨᏓᏨᏣᏛᏬᏍᎠᏨ

If **Chaos** were personified, it would look like the inside of my mind. When I first started working with Laurie K. Grant on organizing my publishing company, I had **Chaos** wrapped around many areas of my business. Her insights coupled with her savvy business skills, helped me to tame the **Chaos** into **CALM** and start a clear path forward with my business. **Carla Wynn Hall, President, Hot Pink Publishing**

ෆ෨ඏ෨ඣ෨ඣ෨ඏ෨

Laurie K. Grant is passionate about, and has made it her purpose, helping women (and men) move forward in their life and business by providing structure, organization, and technology to fit any budget and any lifestyle!! Laurie has created her own business and has worked with many companies including Fortune Top 50 corporations, creating processes to increase efficiency and production.

Laurie's confident, straightforward style, and her many years of experience, can assist anyone in creating a more effective and efficient business. She is the calm amidst the storms of disorganization, lack of processes, and inefficient teams. Laurie can quickly and effectively appraise the situation, recommend changes and solutions, and assist with the implementation!! Laurie can definitely **Create CALM From Chaos**™. **Denise Joy Thompson, Owner, Denise Joy Coaching and The Coach Alliance**

ෆ෨ඏ෨ඣ෨ඣ෨ඏ෨

Laurie K. Grant is truly a master of creating **CALM from** Chaos. She is highly skilled at coaching you through stressful changes. She brings order and **CALM** to even the most chaotic projects. Laurie can help even the most hopelessly disorganized to systemize their business, prioritize conflicting goals, and to bring focus and intention to the forefront. If you need assistance to take control of your business and to develop efficient processes to optimize your effectiveness, Laurie's wisdom will be invaluable to you. **Barb Davies, Online Marketing & Business Consultant, Passionately Organic**

ෆ෨ඏ෨ඣ෨ඣ෨ඏ෨

ACKNOWLEDGEMENTS

There are several people who joined me on this journey to bring this book to you or who assisted me to shift to a new chapter or who have influenced my life. They are highlighted below.

Thank you to **Sandra Strangemore, Owner/Operator, Strangemore Photo,** strangemorephoto.com for the spectacular photos for my book cover and my website.

Thank you to **Anastasia Kravtsova, Anastasia Metro Hair Designs,** anastasiahairdesign.com for the stunning makeover of my hair and makeup for my photos and for teaching me how to recreate this glamourous look.

A big heartfelt thank you to **Sandra Yancey, CEO and Founder, eWomenNetwork, Inc., The Premier Women's Business Network in North America,** new.ewomennetwork.com for believing I was able to SOAR, and I had what it takes to dream and go big.

Thank you to **Susan Brady, the Make 6 Figures Working from Home Coach,** thesusanbrady.com for providing coaching support and encouragement to share my stories and lessons.

I'm grateful to **Margaret Ruff, CPC, ELI. MP, Margaret Ruff Coaching & Consulting,** margaretruff.com, for her belief in my brilliance.

Mega thanks to **Carla Wynn Hall, President, The Soulful Pen,** thesoulfulpen.com for giving me the idea I **Create CALM From Chaos**^{TM}, giving me the opportunity to polish my writing skills and showing me I teach how to **Create CALM From Chaos**^{TM}.

Many thanks to **Mike Shryer** and **Jennifer Morpaw of iInspire Inc.** iinspireinc.com for opening my world to business opportunities where I help so many others achieve business success.

My gratitude goes to **Cv Pillay - The Celebrity SuccSex Guru, Award Winning Bestselling Author, International Speaker, and Screenwriter** for his ability to journey through and past my mind to touch my soul to allow me to illuminate the world with my soul purpose so I may shine and share my most authentic version of myself with you.

I'm indebted to **Naval Kumar, Author – The Digital Marketing Manifesto, Partner at Brand Marketer** brandmarketer.com for sharing his insightful book with me as it provided guidance on how to craft my book as a tool for you to use over and over again. I'm immensely grateful for his ongoing inspiration and encouragement which kept me on the path to write this book.

Kudos to the great team behind me at **The Raymond Aaron Group**, especially **Cara Witvoet**, my Personal Book Architect, whose encouragement and support was especially valuable during some challenging times with my health.

I thank with all my heart, **Raymond Aaron, New York Times Bestselling Author, The Raymond Aaron Group**, aaron.com for reaching out to connect to me in a time of need, providing ongoing friendship, coaching, and mentoring.

I'm grateful to **Justin Trudeau, Prime Minister, Canada** for creating change in our country and setting an honourable example for the world. Justin-Trudeau

I'm inspired by **Theresa May, Prime Minister of the United Kingdom and Leader of the Conservative Party** for her endeavours to combat injustice in British society. prime-ministers-office-10-downing-street

Lastly, I want to honour the **Queen of England, Queen Elizabeth II** for being an excellent role model. I only aspire to be as gracious. royal.uk

www.ingramcontent.com/pod-product-compliance
Lightning Source LLC
Chambersburg PA
CBHW050116210326
41519CB00015BA/3989